Car Repair

by Dan Ramsey

alpha
books

A Division of Macmillan Reference USA
A Simon and Schuster Macmillan Company
1633 Broadway, New York, NY 10019-6785

This book is dedicated to Brendon Ramsey, who has made our journey more enjoyable. May yours be even more so.

Copyright© 1997 by Dan Ramsey

International Standard Book Number: 0-02-862014-3
Library of Congress Catalog Card Number: 97-073178

99   98   97   3   2   1

Interpretation of the printing code: the rightmost number of the first series of numbers is the year of the book's printing; the rightmost number of the second series of numbers is the number of the book's printing. For example, a printing code of 97-1 shows that the first printing occurred in 1997.

Printed in the United States of America

Director of Editorial Services: Brian Phair
Editor: Matthew X. Kiernan
Production Editor: Phil Kitchel
Copy Editor: Damon Jordan
Illustrator: Judd Winick
Designer: Glenn Larsen
Cover Designer: John Viener
Indexer: Nadia Ibrahim
Production Team: Aleata Howard, Rowena Rappaport, Scott Tullis, Pamela Woolf

Contents

7 Every-Two-Years Car Care: It's That Time Again, Again 71

8 What's Wrong with Your Car: Diagnostics for the Clueless 87

9 Electrical System Repairs: Finding the Spark in Your Ride 95

Introduction

Americans have been in love with their cars for about a hundred years now.

That love affair has been chronicled and fed in many ways. The clearest example of this true love was offered in a classic love-story movie, *American Graffiti*. It illustrated the role that cars play in our growing up. Steve courts Laurie with his Chevy. Terry courts Debbie with the same Chevy. Curt, who drives a tinny foreign car, craves meeting the blonde in the Thunderbird. John and Falfa duel it out in a drag race at sunrise. It's all there: love, lust, bravado, insecurity, and the acceptance that youth struggles with. And it's all greased with 30-weight oil. Cars are part of the love process. For some, they are the love objects until something more human comes along.

American Graffiti was the top-grossing film of 1973. You may also remember 1973 as the year of the first large-scale gasoline shortage. Or you may not…. Cars waited in line for hours to fill up with fuel at any price. Real or contrived, the gas shortage was a wake-up call to the American motorist whose thirst for gas-guzzlers was getting out of hand. Luxury cars of the '50s and '60s were getting single-digit miles per gallon. Some weighed more than 5,000 pounds—that's $2\frac{1}{2}$ tons, folks. They were born in an era of 19-cent-a-gallon-and-a-free-glass gas. But they quickly were speeding to an era of dollar-fifty-gas-and-you're-lucky-if-they-clean-your-windshield.

Our love—and progressive need—for cars also is reflected in other areas of our society. There is hardly an aspect of our daily lives that is not changed dramatically because of the automobile. Without cars, there would be no Burger Kings, freeways, or opportunities to "see the USA in your Chevrolet." Nor would there have been a Gulf War or an Exxon Valdez.

Nowhere is our dependency on the car so clear as in the American pastime called *the commute.* Because of the car, we live beyond walking distance of our jobs and recreations. In many parts of the country, we must pile one to five people in an automobile designed for two to four people, and then join what euphemistically is called *the rush hour.* In most cases, it is neither a rush nor just an hour. Worst of all, some car with deferred automotive maintenance decides that upkeep can no longer be delayed—and stops in the center lane! (Give this book to the driver as you slowly drive by, instead of remarking on parental deficiencies.) The wonderful invention that gets us to and from work also keeps us from doing so.

Unfortunately, the car's growing complexity took the do-it-yourself element out of maintenance and repair. You seemingly need an engineering degree—and a politician's salary—to keep your car on the road instead of all over it.

We're going to fix that!

This book demystifies the common car, clearly describing how it works, what you can do to keep it working, and what you can do when it doesn't work. It might not put any professional mechanics out of a job, but it will certainly reduce the number of unprofessional mechanics who take advantage of car owners they consider "idiots."

Here's how we're going to do it. Chapter 1 will give you an overview of how your car—and everybody else's car—runs. Chapter 2 covers what you can do if it doesn't run: whether to fix it yourself or hire someone. It even covers tools and parts. Chapters 3 through 7 offer an easy-to-follow plan for maintaining your car. Then Chapters 8 through 12 tell you how to make nearly every type of car repair you can think of. You'll find lots of step-by-step instructions written by an ex-idiot with the help of some really good professional mechanics. And last but not least, the glossary. All the words that mechanics use when there are children present. Each is clearly defined. Combine them with the clear illustrations and helpful tips to save yourself some bucks. If nothing else, it will lower your mechanic's intimidation factor. And that will save you some big bucks!

To smooth the road ahead, there are little boxes with special information you can use to impress your car.

Dollar Saver

These sidebars include tips for car consumers on how to keep your wallet from needing frequent repairs.

Mechanic's Tip

These boxes offer tips from professional mechanics on how to keep out of their shop. Nice of them!

Car Speak

These boxes offer clear definitions of *terms*, *acronyms*, and *phrases* that mechanics use to make you think you're an idiot. NOT!

Acknowledgements

There is no way that I can list all the people—and cars—who have contributed to my understanding of automobiles. However, maybe I can start with a list of those who directly contributed to this book. Here goes.

Thanks to Harvey Kelm of Lane Community College, Rolla Vollstedt of Vollstedt Enterprises (and the Indy 500), Martin Lawson of Automotive Service Excellence, and Monica Buchholz of the Automotive Service Association. Thanks also to Christopher Finch for his enjoyable autobiography, *Highways to Heaven* (Harper Collins, 1992), which poetically expresses our love affair with cars. Thanks to Mike Michelsen, Buddy Holiday, and the folks who have helped me with the Continental Mark II Association.

Editorially, thanks to Gary Krebs, Sora Song, Matt Kiernan, Phil Kitchel, Damon Jordan, and auto illustrators Tina Trettin and Jeff Yesh.

And thank you, Jude.

Chapter 1

How Your Car Runs and Other Science Fiction

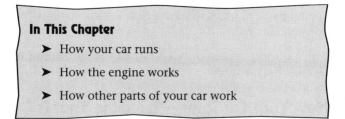

In This Chapter

➤ How your car runs

➤ How the engine works

➤ How other parts of your car work

"Yeah, it looks like the steebenfelz is shot," said the mechanic with the straightest face he could muster. "It'll cost a thousand bucks."

No reaction from the car's dumbfounded owner.

"That's just for parts. Labor will add another fifteen hundred," the mechanic adds and then watches for a reaction.

The car's owner grabs for a nearby wall to brace himself, but doesn't speak.

"Of course, if you want the job guaranteed, you'll need better quality parts—another grand."

Finally, as the car's owner sees his life savings being wiped out by a steebensomethingerother, his wife steps in to the conversation.

"Look, a steebenfelz has nothing to do with the frammerammer acting up. Besides, a new steebenfelz is about 60 bucks, and labor should be little more than an hour. Who are you trying to rip off? Get up, honey, and let's leave this crook!"

"Yes, dear."

Knowing how your car runs can make the difference between a fair repair and a royal rip-off. Mechanics have been known to take advantage of a customer's lack of knowledge, inventing expensive solutions where there is no problem. Finding a qualified and honest mechanic doesn't require luck, it requires a basic understanding of how cars run.

You know you've been ripped off when you see your mechanic on *60 Minutes*.

How Your Car Runs—Assuming That It Does!

In my driveway right now, I have three cars. One is a 1995 Honda del Sol, another is a 1984 Honda Accord, and the third is a 1956 Continental Mark II. As different as these cars are (you could make the two Hondas from the metal in the Continental), they all run using the same laws of nature. They all have many of the same functional parts. The parts may not look the same, but they do the same things.

In fact, the first cars of a century ago and the latest cars have much in common. They both create and control power. My Hondas do it. My Continental does it. Your car does it. Everybody's car does it.

How?

> ➤ Cars create power in the engine.

> ➤ Cars control power with everything else.

Actually, the engine doesn't "create" power. I lied! The engine changes chemical power into mechanical power. Where does it get all this chemical power? Why, from chemicals, of course.

Your car's engine is a place where explosions happen thousands of times a minute. Fortunately, these are controlled explosions—otherwise, you wouldn't get very far before you had to replace your car's engine. These explosions happen when gasoline is ignited inside the engine.

Knowing that, think back to your science class in high school (the one that you slept through, right?). Between snoozes, you learned that a fire requires fuel, air, and a spark to ignite. Sounds about right, but what does this have to do with your car?

Your car's engine changes chemical power into mechanical power by igniting fuel and air, and then using the power from the resulting explosion to move something. Obviously, these little explosions can't directly turn the car's wheels. Other things also have to happen first. And it will take a bunch of explosions to produce enough power to pull away from a stoplight.

So an engine must produce a number of explosions to develop much power—and it must do so in a controlled way so the explosions don't blow up the engine.

We're getting there!

An engine is built so that the explosions are orderly. Your car may have four, six, or eight cylinders. Each cylinder is the place where controlled explosions can occur. Each cylinder (shaped somewhat like an upside-down can) has a solid top and sides, but a movable bottom, called the piston (see the illustration of a cylinder). So, guess what happens when the explosion occurs: The piston moves down.

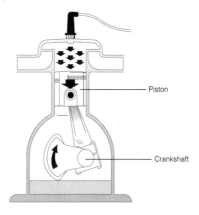

An engine cylinder.

Each explosion pushes the piston downward in the cylinder. A connecting rod at the base of the piston transfers this power to the crankshaft. If you can produce enough controlled explosions in the cylinders, you have rotating power that can (eventually) be used to turn your car's wheels.

Okay, okay. There's a lot more to engine operation than spinning a crankshaft. But that's what happens. That's what gave power to the first cars, and that's what powers your car.

So let's talk about control.

The rest of your car controls the power that your car's engine produces. It starts the engine. It turns the car in the direction you want it to go. It stops your car when you want it to stop.

Yes, there are other parts to your car. The body holds the parts and the people in place. The air-conditioning system keeps people from getting grumpy on long trips (not always successfully). And the radio keeps teenagers' hands busy changing channels. But everything else simply supports the two functions of your car: to create and control power.

If you want, you can stop reading right here and know more than most people know about how their cars run. Or you can keep going and have some more fun learning about your car.

The Infernal Combustion Automobile

Good choice!

Something with as many parts as your car must do more than create and control power. Not much. In fact, once power is created in the engine, control is the operable term. Nobody wants to ride in a car that's out of control!

So let's take a simplified look at the many automotive systems common to all cars. Automotive systems are simply groups of parts that serve related functions. The rest of this section explains each system and how it works with the others in your car.

The next two figures in this chapter show how systems are arranged in a rear-wheel-drive car and in a front-wheel-drive car, respectively. These terms refer to which set of wheels delivers the car's power to the road—rear or front. More on this later.

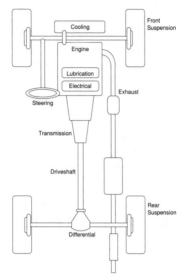

Systems in a rear-wheel-drive car.

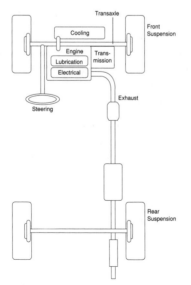

Systems in a front-wheel-drive car.

Fuel System: How Your Car Handles Gas

As you've already seen, the engine needs fuel and air to run. What kind of fuel? Gasoline for most cars, diesel for a few, and propane for even fewer. Most cars run on gas, so that's what I'll talk about.

Gasoline doesn't burn well as a liquid. It must be mixed with air into a vapor that burns easily when ignited. So your fuel system stores the gas in a tank and then pumps it as needed to a carburetor. The carburetor mixes the fuel with the right amount of air and then sends the fuel/air mixture on to the engine to be ignited in the combustion chamber.

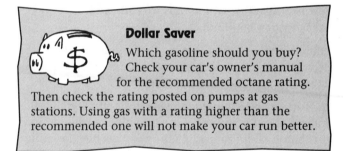

Dollar Saver
Which gasoline should you buy? Check your car's owner's manual for the recommended octane rating. Then check the rating posted on pumps at gas stations. Using gas with a rating higher than the recommended one will not make your car run better.

Your car's fuel system includes the fuel tank, the fuel line, the fuel pump, the carburetor, and filters (see the figure showing the fuel system). Instead of a carburetor, your car may use a fuel-injection system to mix and deliver gas to your engine more efficiently. Some fuel injection systems replace the carburetor while others use injectors at each cylinder. Most cars that are less than a dozen years old have fuel-injection systems.

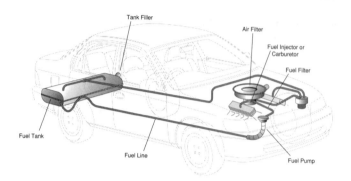

The fuel system.

Ignition System: The Spark in Your Life

Did I mention ignition?

To ignite the fuel/air mixture in the engine's cylinders, an electrical spark must be delivered to the cylinder at the exact second that it's needed.

The battery and alternator provide the electricity, the ignition coil transforms low voltage into high voltage, and the distributor sends the spark to the cylinders (see the figure illustrating the ignition system). Older cars use a mechanical system, called a distributor, to distribute the spark. Newer cars use computers to help manage the ignition in what's called a distributorless or computerized ignition system.

 Car Speak

The ignition system's *spark plugs* are metal-and-ceramic parts that use electricity to ignite the fuel/air mixture in the cylinder. You'll need one spark plug per cylinder when you change them.

Don't worry. There won't be a quiz. For now, just picture how all these systems work and interact.

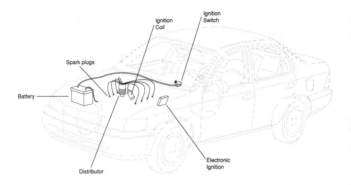

The ignition system.

Cooling System: Keeping Your Cool

With all these explosions happening inside your engine, you'd imagine that it would get hot. It does. In fact, without a cooling system, your engine would soon burn itself up.

Air-cooled engines are designed to be cooled by air flow. But most engines today are water-cooled. Actually, they use a mixture of water and other coolant chemicals to keep the engine's temperature within a safe operating range.

Car Speak

Coolant, a mixture of water and ethylene glycol (named for a famous jazz singer of the '30s) placed in a car's radiator, helps transfer the engine's heat to the air.

The coolant cools the engine by capturing heat from the cylinders without actually entering the cylinders (see the figure showing the cooling system). It does so by flowing through an adjoining chamber called a water jacket. Heat is transferred to the coolant, which is pumped to the radiator through hoses. A fan blows air on the radiator to cool the liquid. The water pump is driven by the rotation of the engine. The fan is driven by the engine on older cars, and an electrical fan is used on newer cars.

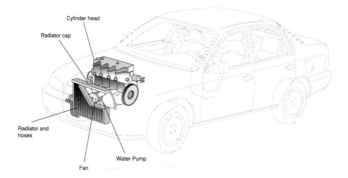

The cooling system.

Cars also can circulate some of that heated coolant through a heater core to warm up the inside of the passenger compartment.

Pretty neat, eh?

Lubrication System: The Well-Oiled Machine

Rub two objects together for a few seconds and you'll see the results of friction: wear. To reduce wear, put some oil or grease between the two objects.

That's how to keep your car's engine from wearing out: Lubricate it well. Inside your car's engine is a system to store, pump, and filter oil that lubricates moving parts.

There are moving parts outside your car's engine as well: wheels, axles, and so on. These parts need a thicker lubricant, called grease.

More cars die young due to poor lubrication than probably any other cause. Save a life: Lube a car! You'll learn how to do this in Chapter 7.

Exhaust System: Waste Removal

The explosions inside your car's engine produce gasses that must be removed to make way for more fuel/air mixture. The exhaust system does this job.

The engine pushes these gasses out through a manifold that collects them from all the cylinders and then pipes them to mix with the outside air. Exhaust gasses transmit the noise created by all these explosions, so the gasses must be muffled (hence, the muffler).

Emission-Control System: Smog Gets in Your Eyes

Nobody likes to smell stinky exhaust air. Nor does anyone want to live with the unburned fuel emissions from cars. So today's cars have an emission-control system that reduces stinky exhaust and emissions before they pollute the air (most of them, anyway).

The catalytic converter is the most famous member of the emission-control family, but there are others. You'll learn who they are and what they do later in this book. You'll also learn how to maintain and even repair slackers.

Transmission System: Getting It in Gear

All that power from the engine must be transmitted to the wheels. In part, this job is done by the transmission system.

Without a transmission, your car probably would have a top speed of about 20 miles per hour. Although that would reduce the number of speeding tickets issued, it wouldn't get you very far very fast.

If you've ever ridden a more-than-one-speed bicycle, you know how gears work. The largest gear gets you going. Then the chain moves to a smaller gear as momentum builds. A car's transmission works in a similar way.

A car's transmission is a box of gears that transmit the engine's power to the driving axle (see the figure displaying the transmission system). It works something like this: First gear transmits the engine's power to move the car from 0 mph to around 20 mph. When shifted to the smaller second gear, the transmission helps the car go from about 20 mph to 40 mph. Third gear, even smaller, moves the car from 40 mph to 60 mph. Fourth gear takes it to as fast as it will go—oops, 65 mph.

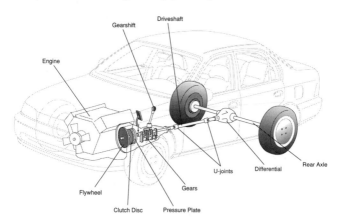

A manual transmission.

A manual transmission requires that the driver press a clutch pedal and move a shifter each time a new gear is needed. Engaging the clutch helps mesh the rotation of the engine and transmission.

An automatic transmission selects and uses the correct gears as needed. A torque converter transfers the power smoothly to the driving axle.

The drive shaft and differential send this power to a rear-wheel-drive car. Front-wheel-drive cars use a transaxle unit to serve the same function, combining the transmission and differential into a single unit.

Yes, that's a pretty simplified description of how an automotive transmission system works. We'll cover the details later.

Electrical System: Batteries Included!

Your car's electrical system is actually a couple of related systems. The starting system starts your car using a battery and starter. The charging system uses the engine's power to drive an alternator, to recharge the battery, and to power accessories. Many other systems within your car then use the battery's electrical energy to operate.

Steering and Suspension System: Turn Left Here! No! Wait!

Imagine a world that didn't allow left turns!

Nowhere on a car is control seemingly more important than in the steering system. Without a steering system, cars can only move straight ahead. The steering system transfers movement of the steering wheel to movement of the tires (see the figure illustrating the steering and suspension systems).

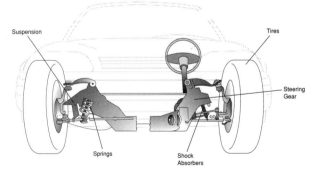

The steering and suspension systems.

A supporting role is played by the suspension system. It absorbs the up-and-down and side-to-side movement of the car as it glides or sputters down the road. Without a suspension system, the road you travel is rougher.

Brake System: Stop Before You Hurt Someone

Imagine a world without brakes!

Commuting would be a world of bumper cars. Travel would be limited by the speed at which you could drag your feet to stop your car. You would have to wear a pair of brake shoes!

Fortunately, cars do have a brake system—and a pretty efficient one at that. Each wheel has a brake controlled by a hydraulic controller called the master cylinder. Power brakes use a booster to make stopping easier. Antilock brake systems (ABS) make sure that braking is smooth and efficient. The emergency or parking brake holds the car in place when parked.

Other Systems: All the Other Junk You Need

There are other systems and components that help your car run. Wheels and tires apply the engine's power to the road. Passenger-restraint systems keep people from becoming projectiles. Entertainment systems, well, entertain. Each system helps make driving cars more efficient, safe, and fun.

Are *you* having fun, yet?

Chapter 2

How to Fix-It-Yourself—
And What to Do with
Leftover Parts

In This Chapter

➤ How to keep car maintenance costs down

➤ Saving money with the right tools

➤ Working safely

➤ Using the CAR maintenance system

➤ Selecting a dealer service shop that takes your plastic, not your body parts

➤ Discovering a really good mechanic without a criminal record

I can't do that! I can't work on my car!

Sure you can!

If you can eat and watch TV at the same time, you can do at least some of the maintenance on your own car—or at least know how to hire someone to do it for a fair price.

The purpose of this chapter is to convince you that you can safely do some or all of your own car's maintenance. It will also help you find professional help for tasks you'd rather not do.

Pickpockets in Overalls

The fact is that the cost of most car repair jobs is about 50 percent parts and 50 percent labor. So that $80 tune-up only required about $40 in parts. In fact, the mechanic also made at least 20 percent more on the parts, because the mechanic buys the parts at a low price and sells them to you at a profit. So you could have done the same tune-up for about $32 in parts and pocketed the rest—if you knew how.

Before you get started taking over the maintenance of your car and saving money left and right, here are some tips to make the job easier and maybe even more fun. Well, at least easier.

> **Tip #1: Buy tools only as needed.** Later in this chapter, you'll learn what tools you need for maintenance and repairs. Some eager folks go right out and buy a $500 set of top-of-the-line tools before they open the hood of their car. Instead, start gathering a few tools needed for basic maintenance, and then build your set as you discover what jobs you want to do and which you'd prefer that others do for you. In most cases, you'll be able to pay for needed tools with savings from the first job you do yourself. Then the tools are yours, free and clear to save you money on future jobs.

> **Tip #2: Buy parts at a discount.** That's not the same as buying cheap parts. Cheap parts are those

made to sell at the lowest possible prices. Discount parts are quality parts that you purchase at less than the suggested retail price—sometimes just a few pennies or bucks more than the cheapies. By learning the year, make, model, and engine of your car, it becomes easier to compare the prices of specific parts by number. You don't have to shop at Wally's Superduper Phantasmagoric Discount Everything Store to get a low price. In fact, you might find a local auto parts retailer who will give you a discount (as much as 35 percent) on purchases of quality parts that will be more durable and reliable. You'll also get knowledgeable answers to your questions—something that Wally's clerks might not be able to offer.

Tip #3: Group maintenance tasks. One way to make your work easier is to do more than one job during a maintenance session. When you check the oil, check the coolant and other fluids at the same time. Use a maintenance plan that helps you use your time efficiently. You'll learn one in this book pretty soon.

Tip #4: Make maintenance a habit. Keeping your car in good condition actually won't take much time at all. In fact, if you make maintenance a regular habit, you can do much of it using the time you'll save by avoiding the frustration of needless repairs. Later in this chapter I'll give you an easy-to-remember method of making car maintenance a habit you can live with.

Where Should I Do It?

One big reason why more people don't do maintenance on their own cars is they just don't seem to have a good place to do it. They think that they need a garage and a shop. Not so. Most car maintenance can be done nearly anywhere the law allows. Next are some ideas about where you can get the work done.

Depending on the task, you might be able to do much of your car's maintenance right where it's parked in the morning. You can open the hood, check and fill engine fluids, and visually inspect your car where it is.

If you're changing oil, you might be able to get permission to drain and replace the oil and filter in the parking lot where you buy the parts. Of course, you'll need an oil-collection can to eliminate spillage and allow recycling. But many auto parts stores can sell you the collection system and even help you recycle the old oil and filter. The same can be said for refilling other engine fluids.

What about maintenance in colder or wetter climates? Some cities have do-it-yourself maintenance shops where you can buy and install parts in a heated garage bay—for an hourly fee. Or you can borrow a friend's garage for a few hours. Or you can do your own maintenance when the weather's nice and have your mechanic do it when it's not so nice.

How Should I Do It?

As you'll soon discover, most car maintenance can be done in a couple of minutes a week and a couple of hours every few months. It's really not going to take that long once you know what you're doing and how to do it.

1. **Plan what you'll do.** The CAR Maintenance System described later in this chapter will help you with that task.

2. **Gather the needed fluids and parts.** Having a system also will help you make sure you have what you need for normal maintenance. Chapters 3 through 7 give you step-by-step instructions and suggest what fluids and parts you'll use.

3. **Gather the tools you'll need for the mainte-nance procedure.** What tools? This is a good time to look over the scads of tools found in an auto parts store and figure out which ones you'll need—and which ones you won't. Let's do that right now.

It's Tool Time!

Tools are simply extensions of your hands. If you had eaten sufficient spinach when you were younger, you wouldn't have to use tools to loosen bolts—you could do it with your bare hands. You didn't, so tools are a must. (Fortunately for toolmakers, few of us liked spinach.)

Cars stay together because of fasteners. Bolts, screws, clips, and other fasteners are used to attach car parts to each other so they work together. Most of the tools you will need for maintaining your car simply tighten or loosen these fasteners. A few perform related functions. The best tools to have are listed here. Let's take a quick look…

➤ Wrenches or sockets move bolts.

➤ Screwdrivers move screws.

➤ Pliers grab parts.

➤ Lubrication or lube tools lubricate parts.

For now, that's about all you'll need. So let's start selecting tools for your maintenance toolbox.

Wrenches

Wrenches come in two sizing systems: SAE and metric. What's the difference? SAE is an acronym for Society of Automotive Engineers. These fine folks established a stan-dard for parts and fluids for American-made cars. Tools that fit these parts are labeled SAE, standard, or U.S. and are sized in fractional inches such as $^3/_8$ inch. Metric is what the rest of the world uses, including European and Asian auto manufacturers. Metric parts and tools are measured in millimeters (mm).

Because there are two common sizing systems for cars sold in the U.S., many tool sets include wrenches for both systems. A $1/2$-inch bolt is just a bit larger than a 12-mm bolt, so the tools are not interchangeable. If you own and maintain only Japanese, German, Korean, or other metric cars, you'll need only metric wrenches. If you have only older American cars, you may need only SAE wrenches. But if you own—or plan to own—cars that use either system, you eventually will need a set of both. Keep them separate, though, so you don't mangle a bolt by using the wrong size wrench. I keep one tray in my tool box for SAE tools and another for metric. The third tray is for my lunch.

An end wrench is a flat-handled tool of hardened steel with an opening at each end. The opening is designed to grasp the outside edges of a bolthead so that it can be turned by rotating the wrench handle. Some wrench ends are open on one side so that the wrench can be slipped around the bolthead. These are called open-end wrenches. The ends of others, called closed-end or box wrenches, encircle the bolthead to get a better grip.

An open-end wrench applies its force on two sides of the bolt. A closed-end wrench applies its force to the corners of a bolthead. The closed-end wrench gives you better grab to turn the bolthead. In addition, a closed-end wrench has six or 12 notches to make it twice as easy to find six corners of the bolthead to grasp.

Some end wrenches have an open end and a closed end, both of the same size. These are called combination wrenches. Other wrenches have both open ends or both closed ends, but of slightly different sizes, such as $1/2$ and $9/16$ inch.

A cousin of the open-end wrench is the adjustable-end wrench. It was made popular by the Crescent Tool Co., so the adjustable-end wrench often is called the Crescent wrench. Because the jaws of an adjustable wrench only contact two sides of the bolthead and because one of the jaws is movable, the adjustable-end wrench isn't as powerful as the closed-end wrench. Even so, every toolbox should have one or more adjustable-end wrenches.

Another relative of the end wrench is the ratchet wrench. The ratchet wrench is a closed-end wrench in which the end can rotate. A locking device called a ratchet makes sure that it only rotates in one direction. To make the ratchet wrench turn bolts in the other direction, simply turn it over.

Socket Wrenches

From the ratchet wrench, it's a simple progression to the socket wrench. A socket wrench is a socket and a separate driver. The socket is a round cylinder that surrounds the bolthead. The socket is named for the size of the bolt it fits: $3/_8$ inch, $9/_{16}$ inch, 21 mm, and so on. The driver is a ratchet handle with a square tip that fits in the end of the socket. The driver is named for the size of this square tip: $1/_4$-inch, $3/_8$-inch, or $1/_2$-inch driver.

Which socket wrench set should you buy? Consider $1/_4$-inch socket wrenches for fasteners on electrical equipment, $3/_8$-inch for most other nonengine car care, and $1/_2$-inch if you plan to take apart an engine or transmission. Folks usually buy a $3/_8$-inch socket wrench set to handle most car maintenance tasks.

Spark plugs require a longer socket than most boltheads. You can buy a spark plug socket to fit a $3/_8$- or $1/_2$-inch driver. The most popular size of spark plug socket is $13/_{16}$ inch (21 mm).

The big brother of the socket wrench is the torque wrench. Bolts and nuts that need to be tightened to a specific pressure (measured in foot-pounds) need this wrench with its special long-handled driver with a torque-measuring device. The device can have a gauge, a scale and pointer, or a dial. You won't need a torque wrench for many tasks, but, if you get into the car-fixing hobby, tell Santa you want one. He probably delivers quite a few each year without getting torqued.

Screwdrivers

Screws are common fasteners for attaching or adjusting car parts. Some screws fasten body parts together. Other screwheads are used to adjust the amount of fuel that is dumped into a carburetor, for example.

Screwdrivers are alcoholic beverages mixed to make your head rotate. They are also tools for turning screwheads. The tip of the screwdriver is designed to fit snugly into the screwhead. The handle of the screwdriver then is turned to rotate the screw.

Screwdrivers are available in many tip designs and sizes that work with corresponding screwheads. Most popular are the straight or standard tip (a.k.a. flathead) and the Phillips or cross tip. Hex-head or Allen wrenches are used to turn hex-head screws—screws with a six-sided hole in the screw head.

Pliers

Pliers grip things. Pliers shouldn't be used to turn bolt-heads (because it's hard to keep a firm grip and you could slip and "round" the bolthead). They can be used to hold a nut while the bolthead is turned (or vice versa), but two wrenches are better. Pliers can grasp and remove a clip fastener or another part. Some pliers have blades that can cut wires. Others compress or crimp electrical connectors.

For all-around use, make sure that you have one pair of slip-joint pliers and one pair of needle-nose pliers in your maintenance toolbox. Slip-joint pliers let you widen the jaws to grasp larger objects, as needed. Needle-nose pliers have long, pointed jaws that can grasp small parts and hold them in place.

Your toolbox also should have a pair of locking-jaw pliers. They sometimes are referred to as Vise-Grips for the name of the company that first made them popular.

Lubrication Tools

Car maintenance often means replacing fluids and lubricants. A grease gun holds cartridges of grease lubricant. You snap the tip of the grease gun around a lubrication or zerk fitting and then squeeze the handle to force grease into the fitting.

A filter wrench helps you grasp and turn an oil filter for removal.

Other lubrication tools help you pour oil into an engine. A small oil can helps you lubricate parts needing light-weight oil. A tube or spray can of white grease lubricant can be used to lubricate door, hood, and trunk hinges.

Other Maintenance Tools

There are many other tools you eventually may want in your trouble-free maintenance toolbox.

➤ A **jack** can lift your car so that jack stands can be placed under it to give you safe room to work under your car. Make sure your car still has the original or a replacement jack. Alternatively, use maintenance or wheel ramps onto which you drive your car to raise one end.

➤ A **tire pressure gauge** makes it easy to check the air pressure in tires without having to drive to the gas station.

➤ A **voltmeter** can help you check out electrical wiring and components in your car.

➤ A **tachometer** can help you set your engine's idle speed.

Don't Be on the Six O'Clock News

We've all heard horror stories about the guy who was crushed while working on his car. I think the story is perpetuated by mechanics who need more work. Yes, it can happen. You can be injured while working on your car. You also can be injured while driving your car, but that doesn't stop you from doing so.

Here are some common-sense rules for safely working on and around your car:

➤ **Cars roll.** When you work on your car, make sure that the parking brake is set. If it isn't reliable or if you'd rather be safe than sorry, wedge a rock or piece of wood in front of and behind one tire. Test it by pushing on one or both ends of the car to verify that it doesn't move.

➤ **What goes up must come down.** If you use a jack or other device to lift your car off the ground, place something under the car to ensure that it will not fall from its perch. The best device for this is a set of two car stands, purchased at an auto parts retailer for about $25. Buy ones that are rated high enough to safely hold your car. Follow directions on the box. Of course, make sure that the jack you're using is placed on a flat and firm surface. If you can't, don't!

➤ **Batteries are powerful.** Your car's battery uses the chemistry of lead and acid to store electrical energy. Older batteries had caps that could be removed, which enabled you to let the acid out. Today's maintenance-free batteries are sealed. Even so, they can develop a leak or vent gases that can explode. This isn't meant to scare you but to help you develop a healthy respect for the power of your car's battery. Wear eye protection and rubber gloves when working around a battery. Respect the electrical current the battery stores. If it can start your car's engine, it can speed up your heart.

➤ **Electronics are sensitive.** Automotive computers operate on just a few volts of electricity. Some use less than one volt. So if they come into contact with 12 volts from the car battery, they can be damaged. In Chapter 9, you'll learn how to jump-start your car to minimize potential damage to your car's electronics and yourself.

➤ **Gas is a combustible fuel.** Inside your engine, gas and air combine with a spark to make an explosion. Outside your engine, the same thing can happen. Make sure that you store fuels in an enclosed container. Oily or fuel-soaked rags must be stored in vented, enclosed containers. Also make sure that you work in a well-ventilated area.

➤ **Don't let the engine bite you.** A running engine has belts and blades and other moving things that can grab you or the clothing you're wearing. The best rule is not to work on a running engine. If you must, identify hot surfaces and moving parts—and stay the heck away from them. Also don't work on a running engine inside a building because carbon monoxide gas can literally take your breath away. If you think mechanics are expensive, wait till you get the doctor's bill!

The CAR Maintenance System

I've been promising you a system that can make maintenance easy to remember. It's time to deliver on my promise.

The easiest way to memorize something is to picture it. You obviously can picture a car. The second-best way to remember is to find an acronym or letters that stand for words. So here goes my system.

There are three types of maintenance on your car:

➤ Check your car.

➤ Adjust your car.

➤ Replace fluids and parts.

The first letters of these three maintenance procedures can be remembered as the acronym C-A-R.

Hang on, it gets easier.

Car maintenance should be performed on a regular basis:

➤ Fluids should be checked about every week.

➤ Adjustments should be made about every six months.

➤ Fluids and parts should be replaced every year or two.

These guidelines fit most modern cars. Cars older than about 25 years will need more frequent adjustments and replacements, depending on age and how much they are driven. Some will need monthly adjustments and yearly replacements.

So let's put these facts together in an easy-to-remember list:

➤ Check your car every week and every three months.

➤ Adjust your car every six months.

➤ Replace fluids once a year and parts every other year.

Check what? Adjust what? Replace what? I knew you would ask. The next section of this chapter will help you find a good mechanic for the car-care jobs you don't want to do. Then, I'll devote an entire chapter to the specifics of each of these maintenance tasks. I'll include a description of each task with step-by-step instructions on how to do it.

These chapters (3 through 7) also group maintenance tasks by where they are done. Those marked with an (H) are done by opening the *hood*. The (U) means that the maintenance step requires you to get *under* the car. A (B) means you will do the job *beside* the car. This system not only helps you work more efficiently, but it also identifies which jobs require you to get under the car—jobs you might prefer to have a mechanic do for you.

The HUB acronym is cute, but has no significance other than it's easier to remember than VQMLTZPVXS.

Finding an Honest Mechanic

Trouble-free car care doesn't mean that you have to do it all yourself. It means doing as much as you feel comfortable with and finding a trustworthy mechanic (or several mechanici, the plural form) to do the rest. Understanding how your car runs and knowing what's involved in its maintenance and repair are important steps in finding a good mechanic and knowing when to hire him, her, or it to do the work.

It's your choice. And your choice is based on understanding your car and your own preferences. This book gives you the information you need to choose and find qualified, reasonably priced mechanical help when you need it. In addition, here are some proven tips for finding a good mechanic.

➤ Look for ASE and other certification programs for automotive technicians.

➤ Ask for the hourly shop rate and compare it with that from dealer shops and other automotive service shops. A shop rate that is too low will tell you as much as one that is too high.

➤ As with dealer shops, take your car in for minor service and watch how it's done. Watching the mechanics at work will tell you much about their knowledge and attitude.

➤ Ask the service manager how much of the work is done by trainees or apprentice mechanics. Is the hourly shop rate for apprentices lower than that for experienced mechanics? It should be.

➤ Ask your friends and neighbors for recommendations about independent mechanics. You'll also get horror stories. From these, you can better decide which mechanics to consider and which to avoid.

What can you do if you're not satisfied with the work done by a mechanic? First, complain to the service manager or owner. If you don't get satisfaction, contact the local Chamber of Commerce to find out what options you have. Some chambers have a grievance committee. Others will refer you to a local or regional Better Business Bureau. Another option is to file a small-claim suit against the shop. By doing a little research in advance, you probably won't have to take it that far.

Dollar Saver

Don't buy cheap! The difference between a good lube job and a cheap one is about five bucks—or a thousand bucks. A lube shop that uses low-grade oil or filters, or hires untrained people who forget to tighten the drain plug, can cost you a thousand bucks for a new engine. Don't shop for the lowest price. Shop for the best value.

Chapter 3

Once-a-Week Car Care: On the Road to Staying on the Road

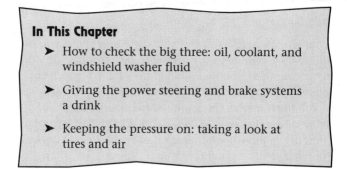

In This Chapter

➤ How to check the big three: oil, coolant, and windshield washer fluid

➤ Giving the power steering and brake systems a drink

➤ Keeping the pressure on: taking a look at tires and air

This is where pride of ownership really begins. People who consider themselves car klutzes have miraculously been transformed into auto aficionados by the simple process of weekly car care.

It's a wonder what a little engine oil on the fingertips can do to bond man and machine. So let's get started.

The first step in the CAR Maintenance System outlined in Chapter 2 is performing simple checks of your car's systems once a week. They're easy to do and can save you thousands of dollars in unneeded repairs. They also offer you peace of mind.

Every Seven Days or Once a Week— Whichever Comes First

Got a couple of minutes? That's all it will take once a week to make sure your car is in good shape. In fact, it will take less time to check your car every week than to worry about it.

Your car uses fluids. These fluids include oil, coolant, windshield washer fluid, brake fluid, and maybe power steering fluid. Your car also uses pressurized air to keep tires inflated. These fluids can evaporate, deteriorate, or leak. In each case, they must be checked and replaced as needed. That's something you can do on a regular basis to help keep your car trouble-free.

Your weekly checks can easily be done over the weekend or before you drive to work on Monday morning (or whenever your workweek starts). If you don't drive your car very often—maybe it's your second car—you can check the fluids and pressure less frequently. But make a habit of it either way. Make your checks on the 1st and 15th of the month, or on even-numbered Wednesdays, for example. If you'd rather watch the odometer than the calendar, make these checks after every 250 miles of driving. Or you can make these checks every time you fill your gas tank.

You might not need tools for these checks. These are mostly visual checks. You might need a wrench or pliers to open a power steering or brake fluid reservoir—but probably not. You will need an air-pressure gauge to check pressure in your car's tires, but you probably can borrow one from a service station attendant. By keeping a rag in the trunk or under your car's seat, you can make sure that you don't get your hands dirty as you make these checks.

You can perform these checks just about anywhere. Some people do it in their garage. Others do them in the driveway or in the parking lot after work. You should be able to efficiently complete these weekly checks in just a few minutes. To ensure that fluids are settled (and you don't get burned), make sure that your engine isn't hot.

To make the process easier, the weekly checks are described in the rest of this chapter in a logical order. First, check fluids under the hood; an (H) in a section title indicates that section covers items under the hood. The next figure shows where to find various fluid reservoirs under the hood. Then check the car's tire pressure, as described in the section marked with a (B) in the title (for beside the car). Always check liquids when the car is sitting level.

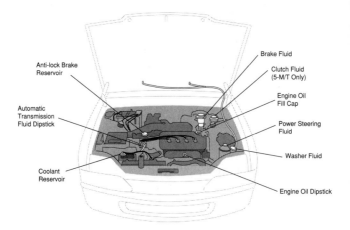

Where to look for fluids.

Check Oil Level (H)

Parts in your car's engine rotate at tremendous speeds. Oil is circulated in the engine to lubricate these parts and keep them from wearing out. When the engine is off, this oil settles to the lowest spot—the oil pan. An oil pan stick or dipstick was installed on the engine by the manufacturer to allow you to check the level of the oil.

Warning: Don't attempt to check your oil in a white tuxedo or a wedding gown!

To check the oil level in your car, follow these steps:

1. Make sure that your car is level. Open the hood and look for the dipstick. It is a rod with a curved handle sticking up from one side of your engine. Push the dipstick down in its tube, if needed, to make sure that it accurately measures the oil level in the oil pan. Have an old rag in hand to wipe the dipstick.

2. Pull the handle up to remove the dipstick rod from the engine. There should be a light or dark brown liquid coating the last couple of inches on the rod. Hold the rod away from your fine clothes to make sure that oil doesn't drip on them. (If the liquid is reddish-brown, you have the automatic transmission dipstick. Replace it and keep looking for the engine oil dipstick.)

3. At the lowest end of the dipstick rod will be marks and maybe the word FULL. Lower on the rod will be another mark and maybe the word ADD. Some dipsticks only have a narrow area that is stamped with a crisscross design or just two dots. If so, the highest point of the design indicates FULL and the lowest point means ADD. Visually check to identify the highest point on the stick covered by oil. This point should be somewhere between the FULL and ADD words or marks.

4. If the top edge of oil is above the ADD mark, the oil level is okay. If the top edge of oil is below the ADD mark, you must add oil without overfilling it. How much? For most cars, the distance between the ADD and FULL lines is about one quart of oil. So you can add one quart of oil. If the oil mark is well below the ADD mark, put one quart in, let it settle a few minutes, and then recheck the oil once.

5. To add oil, first find the oil cap on the engine. Some cars have a twist-off cap on the valve cover (a long and wide part on top of the engine that often has a design or lettering). Other cars have an oil-filler tube with a round cap that you should pull off. To make sure that this is the right place to put oil, remove the cap and look for signs of dark brown oil buildup.

6. Remove the cap from the oil container and carefully pour oil into the engine. If this can't be done without spilling oil on the engine, use a funnel. (Oil won't hurt the outside of the engine, but it smells awful once the engine gets hot.)

7. Wait a few minutes until the oil settles into the oil pan, and then recheck the oil level to make sure that it is between the ADD and FULL marks. Filling oil past the FULL mark can cause more harm to an engine than running it too low. Why? Because excess oil is worked up into a lather by moving parts, reducing the oil's lubrication qualities.

Believe me, it takes longer to describe the process of checking the oil than to do it. Once you've done it for yourself, you can do it again once a week or every 250 miles in less than a minute.

Check Coolant Level (H)

Another important fluid in your car is the coolant. Coolant is a mixture of antifreeze fluid and water that is circulated throughout your car's engine to remove excess heat. The coolant then is circulated throughout the radiator where air flow cools the liquid before its journey back through the engine.

To check the radiator coolant level, follow these steps:

1. Make sure the engine and radiator are cool. If not, wait until they are before checking coolant level.

2. Open the hood and find the radiator. It's typically located at the front of the engine compartment just behind the bumper. On most cars, a coolant reserve tank located nearby holds the top layer of coolant from the radiator. If so, look at the side of the coolant reserve tank for two lines: one identifies MAX (maximum) levels, and one identifies MIN (minimum) levels. The highest level of coolant should be between these two marks.

3. If coolant is low, turn the radiator cap counterclockwise one-quarter turn to relieve any pressure remaining in the cooling system. Then push the cap down and turn it counterclockwise until it is off.

4. Check the coolant level in the radiator. If it is below the base of the filler neck, add coolant (remember: half-antifreeze and half-water), and then replace the radiator cap.

5. Open the cap on the coolant reserve tank and add coolant until the level is between the minimum and maximum marks. Replace the tank cap. Store coolant in a safe and secure place away from progeny and pets.

Check Windshield Washer Fluid Level (H)

Okay, let's do a real easy one. Most cars have an apparatus to spray a soapy liquid on the windshield by pushing a button inside the car. This windshield washer fluid is stored in a reservoir or container under the hood of your car. Not as critical as the oil, but running out of washer fluid can make it difficult to see through a dirty windshield.

To check the windshield washer fluid level in your car, follow these steps:

1. Find the windshield washer fluid reservoir. It is typically a clear or white plastic container holding a pint to a quart of colored liquid. The reservoir may look like a milk jug or a jar.

2. Visually check the fluid level. Some reservoirs have a mark on the side indicating the full level. If not, an inch or two below the top of the reservoir is the full level. Never fill the reservoir to the top because the liquid may expand with weather changes.

3. If the reservoir is less than one-half full (or one-half empty, depending on your view of life), open the top of the reservoir, fill it with windshield washer fluid, and replace the top. Some reservoir tops snap on and off, whereas others are screwed on and off.

What should you fill the reservoir with? You can buy replacement windshield washer fluid at nearly any large store for about a dollar a gallon. Or you can make your own using water and a windshield washer concentrate such as 20/20. Or you can use a drop or two of liquid dishwashing detergent. However, if you live in a colder climate, opt for the commercial stuff. It also includes ingredients to keep the water from freezing during the winter.

Check Power Steering Fluid Level (H)

Not all cars have power steering. Steering systems have evolved over the years so that power steering is not necessary on many smaller cars. But if your car has it, you should check the power steering fluid level once a week or every 250 miles unless the owner's manual says otherwise.

To check the power steering fluid level, follow these steps:

1. Find the power steering reservoir on your car. Power steering units pump or circulate hydraulic fluid to help you easily steer the car with reduced effort. This fluid is held in a reservoir attached to the power steering pump. On most cars, this pump is rotated by a fan belt at the front of the engine, so that's where to look first.

2. To check the power steering fluid level, remove the cap or top to the reservoir. The cap on some power steering reservoirs has a dipstick attached to the underside, indicating the FULL and ADD levels. Other reservoirs have a mark on the inside of the casing to show where the level should be filled to. *Note:* Power steering fluid expands when hot. That means the level in the reservoir will be higher if the engine has been running recently than if it hasn't. Some power steering dipsticks will be marked for FULL HOT as well as FULL COLD. Check the level when cold, if possible.

3. To add power steering fluid, check your car's owner's manual for the fluid brand recommended by the manufacturer. Then pour fluid into the reservoir as needed to bring it up to the full mark. Don't overfill. That's it. You should check your power steering fluid level weekly or every 250 miles, but you shouldn't have to top it off more than every couple of months. If you do, there's a leak somewhere and repair is in order.

Check Brake Fluid Levels (H)

Brakes are obviously important to your car. Without them, you would run right past where you wanted to stop. Brake systems use hydraulics to magnify the pressure of your foot on the pedal to stop the car. Hydraulic systems, in turn, use hydraulic fluid. In this case, the fluid is called brake fluid. Power brake systems also use a booster to enhance your power to stop the car.

To check brake fluid levels in your car, follow these steps:

1. Find the master brake cylinder. On many cars, look under the hood on the wall between the engine and the driver's area (called the firewall). The power brake booster, a large round unit, may be mounted on it. Some import and older cars have them under the floor below the driver, accessed by moving the carpet to expose a metal plate that is, in turn, moved to uncover the master brake cylinder.

2. Clean off the top of the reservoir before opening it so that crud doesn't fall into it. Then remove the cover from the master brake cylinder reservoir. The cover usually has a four- or six-sided head that can be unscrewed with a wrench.

3. Visually check the level of brake fluid in the reservoir. Make sure that the fluid is up to just below the cover's threads or a FULL mark on the inside of the reservoir.

4. To add brake fluid, make sure that you have a can of brake fluid that you opened within the last year. (At about two bucks a pint, you can afford to throw out older brake fluid and use only the fresh stuff.) The owner's manual will tell you which Department of Transportation or DOT grade to use. With the master cylinder cover removed, carefully pour brake fluid in until the level is about $1/_4$ inch below the top. Replace and tighten the cap.

If the master brake cylinder is empty or nearly empty, you might have to bleed the brakes. For this, you'll need to call the American Red Cross...just kidding. Bleeding (removing air from) the brakes is covered in Chapter 12.

Mechanic's Tip
Brake fluid is really tough on paint jobs. Never should the twain meet.

One more related task: Some cars have a hydraulic clutch booster. This helps your foot move the car's clutch plate or disc. If your car has one, you can check your owner's manual to see where and what to do about it. In most cases, the clutch booster uses brake fluid, so checking the fluid level for that is the same as checking the fluid level for the hydraulic clutch booster.

Check Tires and Pressure (B)

Tires of a few decades ago, called bias tires, needed to be replaced once every year or two. Today's radial tires can, with regular maintenance, last five years (or one year of a teenage driver). Today's tires also are safer and make a car easier to steer when compared to the older, bias tires.

The key statement in the last paragraph is "with regular maintenance." That's where you come in. You either can check the air pressure in your tires or ask the gas station attendant to do it once a week. By doing so, you can make sure that you get 50,000—not 25,000—miles from your 50,000-mile tires. It can also save fuel as underinflated tires reduce fuel economy.

To check tires and pressure on your car, follow these steps:

1. Read your car's owner's manual or the side of a tire to learn what air pressure you should have in your tires, measured in pounds per square inch, or psi. Most modern car tires have a recommended pressure of somewhere between 24 and 34 psi when the tires are cold. A typical recommended cold pressure is 28 psi. Add 2 to 4 psi when carrying a heavy load or pulling a trailer. The tire's maximum load pressure is embossed on the tire wall. Don't exceed it or the tire police will repossess your tread. Actually, excessive pressure makes tires wear unevenly and reduces their usable life.

2. Check tire pressure in your driveway or at a nearby gas station when the tires are not hot from driving. Find the valve stem on the front left (driver's side) tire. It protrudes from the wheel rim. If the valve stem has a cap, unscrew it and set it aside. Place the mouth of your tire-pressure gauge against the end of the valve stem. Push it until you hear a rush of air, and then release it. The tire gauge indicates how much pressure is in the tire on a dial or on a sliding scale.

3. If air pressure is lower than it should be, add air using an air line at a gas station or tire shop, or a hand pump. If pressure is greater than it should be, use the nipple on the tire gauge to press the center of the tire valve stem and release air. Release a little, and then recheck the pressure. Remember to replace the valve stem cap if your tire has one.

4. While you're there, visually inspect the tire for wear. Some tires have a tread indicator that shows you when the tires are too worn to be safe. Inspect the tire for damage as well. A cut in the tire casing can

become an auto accident just a few miles down the road. Wear across the tire tread should be even. If not, take your car into a tire shop—after reading Chapter 12.

5. Repeat this process for the left-rear, spare, right-rear, and right-front tires. This circling of the car makes it easier to remember which tires have been checked if you're interrupted. Don't forget the spare tire.

Why all this ruckus about tire pressure? Because the main reason tires don't live as long as they're designed to isn't high blood pressure; it's low tire pressure. Low tire pressure makes tires wear out at the edges. It also makes the car ride sloppy. Checking tire pressure once a week or every 250 miles is an easy way to increase the life and safety of your tires. And it takes just one or two minutes.

Chapter 4

Once-a-Quarter Car Care: How to Pay for College While You Get an Education

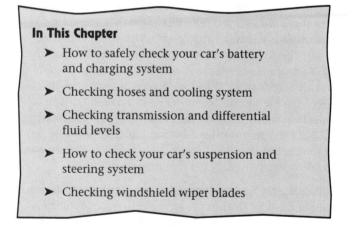

In This Chapter

➤ How to safely check your car's battery and charging system

➤ Checking hoses and cooling system

➤ Checking transmission and differential fluid levels

➤ How to check your car's suspension and steering system

➤ Checking windshield wiper blades

By making the basic checks offered in Chapter 3, you've moved ahead of most car owners and can now sit near the front of the classroom. I'm proud of you—and will be as long as you keep up on your homework!

Once you make these weekly checks a habit, maintenance not only becomes easier, it's more fun. You'll gain a better understanding of your car. And you'll be able to read it more accurately.

The second step in the CAR Maintenance System is performing simple checks of your car's systems once every 3,000 miles and replacing parts as needed. Here's where you can really begin solving car problems before they happen.

Buddy, Can You Spare a Quarterly?

Modern cars have thousands of parts. Some of these parts can wear out or at least need periodic adjustments. You can minimize wear and cost by checking these components and replacing them on a regular basis.

The CAR Maintenance System presented in this book suggests that you check eight different components about every three months or 3,000 miles. (That's 4,800 km for you metric fans.) This chapter describes how to make those eight checks. Of course, the frequency with which you make these checks depends on the age of the car and how much you drive it. Older cars need more frequent checks, even once a month. For newer cars that aren't driven as much, you can get away with checking these components about every six months. However, running down the list will take less than an hour on most cars, so you may want to do it more often. Better safe than sorry, right?

This chapter first presents tasks completed under the hood (designated by an H in the section title), moves on to tasks you handle under the car (indicated by a U in the section title), and then describes tasks that you complete from beside the car (designated by a B in the section title). Again, you don't have to do them yourself. Just make sure you tell the mechanic or lube service which checks you want done. You're the boss!

Check the Battery and Charging System (H)

Batteries store electrical power for starting the car, running the radio, and other necessities. Modern cars use 12-volt batteries; your house uses about 120 volts. Even so, there's still enough power in a car battery to get your attention. The charging system (the alternator and voltage regulator) replaces the used-up electricity. If it doesn't get replaced, your car won't start.

It's very important to work safely around your car's battery. First, the battery uses acid and lead to store electricity. Second, electric current from a battery (at 50 or more amps) can quickly destroy a car's computer system or smaller wires and components. Wear rubber gloves and safety goggles when working around the battery. And make sure that you don't touch metal objects between the battery terminals and other metal.

The only tools you'll probably need are a battery terminal cleaner (a couple of bucks at any auto parts store) and a wrench for loosening bolts. You could use a standard wire brush, but, if you do, don't use it for other cleaning purposes because the battery acid can be transferred to other surfaces.

Also, put that cigarette out first! A flame or spark near a battery—even a so-called "sealed" battery—can cause an explosion. Another documented danger of smoking!

To check the battery and charging system on your car, follow these steps:

1. Identify the terminals. One has a + (positive) on or near it and one has a – (negative). The cable on one of these two terminals is attached to the engine block and the other goes to the starter. The one that goes to the engine is called the ground terminal; this is usually (but not always) the negative terminal.

2. Remove the plastic terminal caps, if there are any, from the ground terminals and carefully brush away any white powder (corrosion). If the battery cables attach to the battery with a nut, remove the nut and clean the terminal and cable end with a wire brush, and then skip to step 6. If the battery uses terminal posts, follow steps 3 through 5.

3. Use a wrench to loosen the bolts at the end of the battery cable where it wraps around the ground terminal. Carefully wiggle the cable end up and down until it comes off the terminal. (If the end doesn't come off the terminal easily, buy and use a battery terminal puller from a parts store.) Then loosen and remove the cable on the other terminal. *Warning:* Striking a terminal or cable end with a hammer to loosen it can loosen the terminal inside, ruining the battery.

4. Place the end of the terminal-cleaning tool over each terminal and rotate it a few times. The wire brush inside the tool will clean the terminal post.

5. Twist and open the terminal-cleaning tool to expose the round wire brush inside. Insert this brush into the cable ends and rotate the tool to clean the inside of the ends. If the cable ends are broken or the wire is frayed, replace the cable with one of the same length.

6. Use an old paint brush or a Christmas gift tie to dust away dirt on the top and sides of the battery. Make sure that the debris doesn't fall on other components or on the car's paint. If the battery is very dirty, remove it from the car and carefully clean it with a solution of a pint of water and a teaspoon of baking soda (season to taste). Make sure that the solution doesn't get inside the battery.

7. If you have one, use a voltmeter ($10 at Radio Shack) to check the battery's voltage. A fully charged battery should read 12.5 to 13.5 volts of power. If it is less, take the battery to a gas station for charging or do it yourself with a battery charger (about $25 to $50). A mechanic's battery charger (a few hundred dollars) also can tell you the condition of the battery and whether it will hold a charge. If it won't, replace it now before you get stranded in a land where batteries cost twice as much.

8. When reinstalling your car's battery, attach the grounded terminal last. Install treated felt washers (from your parts store) under the cable ends to reduce corrosion. Place the cable end over the terminal and then tighten the bolt until the end fits snugly. Don't overtighten the bolt because cable ends are made of a soft metal that can break easily.

Mechanic's Tip

If you hear a clicking sound when you try to start your car, the culprit is probably the battery terminal connections. Clean them as described here. If that doesn't work, have your battery tested and charged or purchase a battery charger and follow the manufacturer's instructions.

Check the Hoses (H)

The most intimidating components on your car are also pretty easy to check and maintain: hoses. Open the hood of your car and you'll see all shapes and sizes of hoses from $1/_2$ inch to 4 inches in diameter. These hoses deliver fuel, circulate engine coolant, move refrigerant, and much more. Check them once every three months and replace them if they seem soft or have cuts in the surface.

To check hoses on your car, follow these steps:

Mechanic's Tip

Be very careful when working around an engine that's running. Engine surfaces quickly become hot to the touch and can burn you. Fan blades and belts are moving quickly and can bite. Mechanics take a moment to look for such dangers before working on a running engine. You should, too.

1. With the engine running, open the hood and begin looking for patterns to your car's hoses. To help define the maze, check the underside of the hood for stickers that serve as a map. You may see stickers labeled Vacuum Hose Routing, Emission Hose Routing, or For Pizza Delivery call 1-800-555-1234. Other hose systems are self-explanatory, going to and from the radiator (cooling system), to the carburetor (fuel system), or to the car's heater (heating system). If hoses are not color-coded, you often can identify families of hoses by their relative size. Vacuum lines, for example, will all be about the same diameter. You often can identify hoses by the end connection as well (see step 3).

2. Inspect each hose, squeezing it to see whether there are any cuts, leaks, or wear. Listen for soft hissing that identifies a loose vacuum line. Look for liquids that identify a leaking hose or fitting.

> **Mechanic's Tip**
> Don't mess with air-conditioner hoses.
> They are pressurized and contain a
> refrigerant gas. If your air conditioning
> system hoses are in poor condition, take
> your car to a licensed air conditioner service shop
> with the tools and training to do the work for you.

3. Check the ends of each hose to make sure they are
securely attached. If not, tighten them. Vacuum
lines usually slip on. Cooling system hoses have
screw clamps on the ends that are tightened with a
screwdriver. Fuel lines often use spring clamps with
tips you squeeze to loosen pressure on the hose.

4. Turn off the engine before replacing any hoses. If
you cannot easily remove a hose from the car to find
a replacement part, take measurements. Remove one
end of the hose, if you can, and measure the inside
and outside diameters. Then measure the length.
Write down any identifying numbers that appear on
the hose, such as TA1-05. If you have a service
manual for your car, look up the part to determine
what it is called.

Check the Cooling System (H)

As you learned in Chapter 1, the cooling system is a critical part of your car. If your engine gets too hot, it can
quickly damage itself. So checking your car's cooling system is an important step in keeping it trouble-free.

Don't mess with hoses on fuel-injection systems. They are
pressurized and contain gasoline. If your fuel-injection
system hoses are in poor condition, take your car to a mechanic with experience in repairing such systems.

To check the cooling system on your car, follow these steps:

1. With the engine cold, open the radiator cap. Some caps require you to lift a lever on the cap that releases pressure. Others are twisted one-quarter turn to relieve pressure. Newer systems might have a cap on a separate coolant reservoir near the radiator instead of on the radiator itself.

2. Visually inspect the cap and clean off any rust deposits. If the cap leaks or is more than a couple of years old, replace it. The cost of a new cap is typically less than $5—a fraction of the cost to replace an engine damaged by overheating.

3. Visually inspect the coolant in the system. The top of the coolant should be near the top of the radiator or near the FULL mark on the coolant reservoir. Fill as needed with a mixture of half coolant and half water. Chapter 7 will show you how to flush your cooling system.

Mechanic's Tip

If your car overheats, cautiously lift the lever on top of the cap to release pressure. After a minute, place a folded cloth over the cap and twist the cap counterclockwise one-quarter turn to relieve more pressure. Wait a moment, then place the cloth over the cap again and remove the cap. Allow the engine to cool 20 minutes before refilling.

4. Inspect the cooling system hoses if you haven't already done so. There are usually two: one between the top and one between the bottom of the radiator

and the engine. Radiator hoses should feel firm and not mushy. Check and tighten the screw clamps on the end of the hoses.

5. Inspect the front and back side of the radiator for debris and damage. Bugs, leaves, papers, and other debris can block the airflow and reduce the radiator's efficiency. Use a soft brush or compressed air to remove debris. Make sure that you don't bend any of the honeycomb fins on the radiator. They allow the passing air into the radiator to keep your engine cool.

6. Inspect the top and bottom of the radiator for small leaks or rusty spots that may soon become leaks. If you find any, take your car to a radiator shop where it can be repaired.

Check the Transmission Fluid (H/U)

Your car either has an automatic (shifts automatically) or manual (you shift gears) transmission. Each uses a fluid or lubricant to keep it healthy. At least four times a year, you should check the fluid level in your transmission to make sure that it is full. You'll need a clean rag to check the automatic transmission fluid from under the hood. You'll need to get under most cars to check the lubricant level in a manual transmission.

To check the automatic transmission fluid level in your car, follow these steps:

1. Make sure that the car is level. Set the car's parking brake and start the engine. When the engine is warm and at idle speed, move the transmission selector through each gear range a couple of times, ending at neutral.

2. With the engine still running, lift the car's hood and look for the automatic transmission dipstick. It looks

like the engine oil dipstick but is located behind a rear-wheel drive engine or above the transmission on a front-wheel drive car. The dipstick often is painted a different color to distinguish it from the engine's oil dipstick.

3. Got it? Pull the transmission dipstick out from the tube and visually check that the fluid is a reddish-brown, identifying it as automatic transmission fluid. Carefully touch the liquid on the end of the dipstick to make sure that it is warm. It should not be hot. Then, using a clean rag, wipe the dipstick clean and replace it in the tube until the dipstick cap seats.

4. Pull out the transmission dipstick again and read the level. Some automatic transmission dipsticks will be stamped with words like MAX. LEVEL HOT IDLING IN NEUTRAL—or not. The safe operating range will be marked.

5. If the automatic transmission fluid is low, add fluid through the dipstick tube. You'll need a special funnel (from your handy-dandy auto parts supplier) to get the fluid into the small tube, but it can be done. Use the type of automatic transmission fluid recommended by the manufacturer. It's probably identified in the owner's manual. If not, ask the auto parts clerk what type is recommended for your car. Add just a little at a time until it is near the top of the operating range shown on the dipstick.

To check the manual transmission lubricant level in your car, follow these steps:

1. Look under your car to find the transmission. On a rear-wheel drive car, the manual transmission is below the floor-mounted gear shifter. On a front-wheel drive car, the transmission or transaxle unit is under

the hood and beside the engine (usually on the passenger side of the car). You might need to safely jack up the car and place stands underneath it in order to find room to work. Because the transmission fluid must be as level as possible when checked, don't raise the car any more than is necessary to get to it.

2. To check the level of fluid in the transmission or transaxle, first find the level plug. It's typically a bolthead on the side of the transmission casing. Use a wrench to turn it counterclockwise and remove it.

3. It's pinky-finger time. The transmission lubricant should be filled up to the bottom of the level plug hole. Insert your smallest finger inside the level plug hole to see if it is so. If not, add the manufacturer's recommended lubricant through the level plug hole until the top of the liquid is at the bottom of the hole.

Check the Differential Lubricant Level (U)

A car's differential includes the gears that distribute the single drive shaft's rotation to two or four wheels. Rear-wheel drive cars have a differential on the rear axle. Front-wheel drive cars include the differential in the transmission, so there isn't a separate differential unit. Four-wheel drive cars use a transfer case to distribute power to all four wheels.

Most car manufacturers recommend that the differential be filled with an SAE 80-90 weight lubricant. Transfer cases for four-wheel drive vehicles typically use a lubricant similar to (but not the same as) automatic transmission fluid. You might need to order this special concoction from the car's authorized dealer. It's refined from pure gold found only in the Andes. Check your car's owner's manual or service manual for requirements.

To check the differential lubricant level in your car, follow these steps:

1. Look under your car to find the differential. On a rear-wheel drive car, the differential is a round, metal case between the two rear wheels. The transfer case for a four-wheel drive car is on either the front or rear axle. If necessary, safely jack the car up and place stands underneath it.

2. To check the level of fluid in the differential or transfer case, first find the level plug. On many cars, it's a bolthead on the side of the casing; use a wrench to turn it counterclockwise and remove it. On some cars, it's a rubber plug on the side of the casing; pry it off with a small screwdriver.

3. Use your finger to check the lubricant level. It should be filled up to the bottom of the level plug hole. If it isn't, add the manufacturer's recommended lubricant until the top of the liquid is at the bottom of the level plug hole.

Check Suspension and Steering (Q)

Problems with your car's steering and suspension come on gradually and might not even be noticed until the system fails. So it's very important that you check these systems every 3,000 miles. Fortunately, it's an easy process that you can do while you're making your other quarterly checks.

To check the suspension and steering on your car, follow these steps:

1. With the car sitting in a level spot, push down on the top of the front left fender and quickly release it. Do the same on the front right fender. You're trying to make the corner of the car bounce as if it just hit

a bump in the road. If the car bounces more than once or twice, the shock absorbers may need replacing. Chapter 12 shows you how.

2. With the front end of the car raised and safely blocked, inspect the steering mechanism underneath the car. Especially look at the shock absorbers for possible fluid leaks. Then ask someone to repeatedly turn the steering wheel left and right as you watch how the mechanism works. Most of it is common sense. Trace the movement from the steering gear box through the rods to the back side of the wheels. Movement should be smooth with no clunks or metallic sounds.

3. From beside a front wheel, grab the tire and move it from side to side. Movement should be smooth and not jerky or noisy. Then grab the tire at the top and bottom, moving it toward and away from you a few times to see whether it seems loose.

4. Now spin the tire and listen for noises. A grinding sound can mean that the wheel bearings need lubrication or the brakes are dragging (see Chapter 12). When you are done, remove the stands and lower the car.

Repairs to your car's suspension and steering systems can be done either by you (see Chapter 12) or by your favorite mechanic. Don't let these repairs go.

Check the Windshield Wiper Blades (B)

Unless you live on Mt. Waialeale on the Hawaiian island of Kauai (where 480 inches of rain fall every year!), your windshield wiper blades probably won't wear out very often. Instead, they will deteriorate from sun exposure. Or they will build up with automotive lubricants thrown up by cars passing in the rain.

Don't wait until a rainy day to check and service your car's windshield wiper blades. Do it as you make your other quarterly checks. Then, when you need them, your windshield wipers will be ready to serve you.

To check the windshield wiper blades on your car, follow these steps:

1. Visually inspect the windshield wiper mechanism for damage or loose parts. Also clear the area around the wiper arms of debris that can slow down their movement.

2. Inspect the windshield wiper blades for tears and other damage. Replace damaged or deteriorated blades with identical blades. Remove them in the auto parts store's parking lot and take them in for a match. Blades and their frame are removed by lifting the arm and unhooking the end of the arm from the center of the blade's frame. Some blades require you to push a button in the center of the frame to release the blade.

3. If the blades are simply dirty, clean them with a mild detergent. Also clean your car's windshield to ensure that elongated but colorful bug carcasses don't obstruct wiper travel.

Chapter 5

Twice-a-Year Car Care: Spring Ahead or Fall Behind

In This Chapter

➤ How to replace oil and filter on your car

➤ Adjusting the carburetor and throttle linkage on older cars

➤ How to increase tire mileage by rotating them every six months

Many car owners will check and replace fluids, but draw the line at making adjustments to their cars. Others see adjustments as another area in which they can save some money and, just maybe, increase their pride of ownership.

This chapter describes the steps you can take every six months or 6,000 miles to keep your car well adjusted. As with other tasks in this book, you can do them yourself, or you can hire others to do them for you. In either case, this chapter will help you understand what needs to be done, why, and how.

It's Halftime

There are thousands of parts in your car. Some just sit there like potatoes, enjoying the ride. Others are hard workers with a mission. Depending on how much they are called upon to work (and how well they were made), these hard-working parts will need to be adjusted every once in a while. On average, once in a while means about every six months or 6,000 miles of driving. Your mileage may vary.

You'll need to break out the toolbox (Chapter 2) for most adjustments: screwdrivers, wrenches, and a few special tools. I'll point them out as you need them.

The remaining sections in this chapter describe the adjustments you may need to make and how to make them. Remember: *H* means under the hood, *U* designates adjustments done under the car, and *B* notes adjustments made beside the car.

Replace that Dirty Oil and Filter (H, U)

Okay, okay. You're technically not adjusting your oil and filter; you're replacing them. But it should be done about every 6,000 miles, so I used my unexpired poetic license to keep this important step in the chapter with other adjustments. Sue me!

An oil filter is simply a can with a paper-like filter in it. Think of it as a can of coffee filters. The oil is forced through the filter, depositing carbon, bits of metal, and other contaminants on the filter's surface. Instead of periodically cleaning the oil filter, you will replace it with a new one—hopefully before the contaminants block the flow of oil through the engine.

Some cars are designed to be run 7,500 miles between oil changes. Others require an oil change every 3,000 to 6,000 miles. How you drive is as important to oil-change frequency as miles. Cars driven only short distances, pulling trailers, or in the mountains require more frequent oil changes than those driven regularly at highway speeds.

Some folks say it isn't necessary to replace the oil filter with every oil change; you can replace the oil filter with every other oil change. Let's think about this for a moment.

When you change oil in a car, you replace all the oil except what's in the oil filter. So about 20 to 25 percent of all the oil in the car will still be dirty. Not only that, the oil filter contains the contaminants filtered from the oil. It's the yucky stuff. The contaminants are not really dirt but carbon from the combustion process. Filters filter the big chunks, which can clog up a filter, making it virtually useless. Three quarts of clean oil plus one quart of dirty oil equals four quarts of dirty oil—and now you've got a filter that doesn't filter!

Okay, let's weigh this against the cost of a new oil filter: less than five bucks (less than three bucks for many cars). So here's the new rule I ask you to follow:

> **Always change the oil filter when you change the oil.**

On behalf of your car, thanks!

In addition to getting an oil filter for the oil change, you need oil! How much oil? Look in the owner's manual. It may say something like oil capacity: (or crankcase capacity) 3.5 L (3.7 qt.) including filter. Oil containers usually have marks on the side to indicate milliliters (ml) or ounces (oz).

To replace the oil and filter on your car, follow these steps:

1. Make sure that your car is parked in a level spot. Start your car and let the engine run for about 15

minutes to warm up the oil. Warm oil drains more thoroughly and brings with it more built-up sludge. Use this time to gather the tools you'll need: a wrench (to remove the oil pan plug), an oil-draining pan, and an oil filter wrench. Rubber gloves will keep warm oil off your skin. Shut off the engine when you're ready to start. Wait about five minutes for the warm oil to drain to the lowest spot in the engine, the oil pan.

2. Place the drain pan under the oil pan plug. The plug has a bolthead and is located at the lowest point underneath the engine. If necessary, jack up the car and install safety stands. Using a wrench, turn the plug counterclockwise to loosen it. Set the plug and washer aside for later. Alternatively, you can use a hand-operated oil siphon to draw oil from the oil pan through the dipstick tube without having to crawl under the car.

3. After all oil is drained into the pan, reinstall the old plug and a new washer (if so equipped) on the oil pan. Tighten the plug with a wrench. Don't forget this step or your car's engine could be ruined by operating as oil drips out the bottom. It would bleed to death.

4. Move the pan to below the oil filter. On some engines, the oil filter can be reached from under the hood. Others require that you remove it from underneath the car. If necessary, jack up the car and install safety stands. Be careful when working around the underside of your car because the exhaust pipe and other components are hot.

5. Using an oil filter wrench, twist the filter counterclockwise two or three turns. Oil should begin dripping from the filter to the pan. Use your hand to rotate the oil filter until it comes off the shaft. Then

tilt the filter so that oil in it can drain into the drip pan.

6. Make sure that the new oil filter is the same size as the old one. Open a can of new oil, get some oil on the end of a rag or your finger, and spread it around the circular rubber seal on the end of the new oil filter. Place the new oil filter on the screw-on filter shaft and turn it clockwise. Tighten the new filter by hand only, about two-thirds of a turn after the gasket makes contact with the filter holder. Don't tighten the filter with the oil wrench.

7. Replace the oil by following the instructions in Chapter 3 on checking oil level: find the oil filler location and use a funnel to pour in the appropriate amount of oil, and then recheck the oil to make sure that it is between the ADD and FULL marks.

8. Replace the oil filler cap securely. Wipe off all tools with a clean rag and put them away for later use. Make sure that you take the used oil to a recycling center or an auto parts store to have it properly disposed of. If you DON'T recycle oil properly, a large fellow with long, hairy arms will recycle you!

Check your oil level after your next short drive. Make sure that the oil level is within range: above ADD and below FULL on the dipstick. Add oil as needed. Also look under the car to see whether there are any new oil drips, indicating that the oil plug or oil filter is not tight.

Adjust the Carburetor (H)

If your car has a fuel-injection system instead of a carburetor (refer to your owner's manual), there's not much you can or have to adjust. Fuel is regulated by an electronic signal from your car's computer. Fuel injection systems are covered in Chapter 10.

The carburetor is an important part of many cars over a decade old. It mixes the right amount of fuel and air to make a combustible vapor that your engine's spark plugs can ignite. The adjustments you can make are the ratio of fuel to air (rich or lean) and the amount of fuel fed to make the engine operate when the car isn't moving (at idle).

Most newer carburetors are sealed at the factory and don't allow owner adjustments. So you can spend the time required to adjust the carburetor doing something else. If you have an older car and need to adjust the carburetor, however, here's how to do it:

1. Attach a tachometer to your car's engine following the manufacturer's directions—unless your car already has a tach in the instrument cluster on the dashboard. Tachs measure the engine's operating speed in revolutions per minute (rpms).

2. Start the engine and let it run for about 15 minutes to warm it up. Look it over. You're looking for screwheads that can be turned to adjust the idle speed and the idle mixture. *Hint:* The idle speed screw is at the end of the throttle linkage and at the side of the carburetor, whereas the idle mixture screw (or screws) is on the carburetor itself.

3. To adjust the idle speed, you'll be using the tachometer to set the engine's speed at idle. Your car's owner's manual will tell you what that speed should be. Or there may be a sticker on the inside of your car's hood that indicates the idle speed. For many cars, idle speed is 500 to 750 rpm. Using a screwdriver, turn the idle speed adjustment screw clockwise to increase rpms or counterclockwise to decrease rpms. If your carburetor has an idle solenoid adjustment, you'll need to make a second adjustment for a high idling speed. There are many

carburetor designs out there. Follow instructions in your car's service manual for this adjustment.

4. To adjust the idle mixture, make sure that the tachometer is connected to the engine to tell you its operating speed. Find the idle mixture adjustment screws on the carburetor (underneath the air cleaner). A single-barrel carburetor (on smaller or older cars) has one idle mixture screw, whereas a two- or four-barrel carburetor has two screws. Turn the screw(s) in, or clockwise, until the engine is at its lowest speed. Then turn them out, or counterclockwise, until further turning doesn't increase speed. That's the best mixture for the idling speed. Do this a couple of times to get the best mixture, especially if your car has two idle mixture adjustments.

Adjust Tire Rotation (B)

Car tires are literally where the rubber meets the road. As they roll their way to your destination, they also wear out. Old bias tires would wear out in 10,000 to 20,000 miles. New radials last four times as long—unless they don't wear evenly. It's easy to reduce uneven tire wear by making sure that tires are inflated properly (see Chapter 3) and rotated or moved to different positions on the car to equalize wear (forthcoming).

Not all car and tire manufacturers recommend rotation. Some suggest that tires should be replaced when they are worn, without first trying to rotate them. Tests have shown that rotation doesn't prolong tire life; it only makes them wear more evenly among the four tires. They suggest that front tires frequently wear differently than rear tires (which is why they are rotated) so they should be replaced as a set. The rear tires also should be replaced as a set when worn. Check your car's owner's manual for the tire rotation pattern, if any, suggested for your car.

The only tools you'll need for the job are those that (hopefully) came with your car: a jack and a lug wrench, also known as a tire iron.

To rotate the tires on your car, follow these steps:

1. Safely jack up and place stands under all four wheels of your car. If you cannot lift all four wheels, jack up and place stands under one side of your car or the other.

2. Remove wheels as needed, reinstalling them on the car for the most even and efficient wear, as recommended by the car's owner's manual.

For front-wheel-drive cars and front-engine, rear-wheel-drive cars with radial tires, move the front left tire to the left rear and vice versa. Then move the front right tire to the right rear and vice versa.

For front-engine, rear-wheel-drive cars with bias-ply tires, move the front left tire to the rear right, the rear right to the front right, the front right to the rear left, and the rear left to the front left wheel. Got that?

If your car's spare tire is a standard tire (rather than one of those weird spare-only tires that look like a large chocolate doughnut), you might want to rotate it among the others. If so, rotate as recommended by the manufacturer.

Tires should wear evenly, with approximately the same amount of tread at the center as near the edges. If the edges wear faster, the tire probably is underinflated. If the center wears faster, the tire may be overinflated. The solution to either problem is to check tire pressure weekly, as described in Chapter 3. If one edge of a tire wears faster than the other, the wheel alignment (Chapter 12) probably is incorrect and should be checked by a wheel-alignment shop.

Chapter 6

Once-a-Year Car Care: Or Every 12 Months— Whichever Comes First

In This Chapter

➤ How to adjust ignition timing on older cars

➤ Replacing drive belts that keep your car running smoothly

➤ Lubricating your car's chassis—or having it done for you

Everybody still with me?

Back in Chapter 3, "Once-a-Week Car Care," you learned to check your car's fluids on a weekly basis. Well, 52 of those weekly checks have come and gone and it's time to replace some of those fluids. And some parts, too.

Why replace them? Automotive fluids are your car's blood, sweat, and tears. They are the fluids that circulate and lubricate within your car. Every once in a while, they need to be removed and replaced with new fluids. At the same time, there are automotive parts that need replacement about every 12 months.

This chapter offers instructions on how to replace automotive parts and fluids annually. Of course, there are so many car designs and needs that there can't be a hard-and-fast rule for much of anything having to do with cars. So read your car's owner's manual, apply your common sense, ask your mechanic, and determine when your car needs parts and fluids replaced.

You'll need your handy-dandy toolbox (Chapter 2) to replace parts. I'll point them out as you need them.

Don't forget: *H* means under the hood, *U* designates adjustments done under the car, and *B* denotes adjustments made beside the car. There will be a quiz on this later.

Readjust the Ignition Timing (H)

An engine is poetry. Maybe it's not Carl Sandburg, but it's got meter. At the exact moment that fuel is compressed in the combustion chamber, a spark comes along to ignite it. So the timing of the ignition is critical. Without correct ignition timing, power is lost.

The purpose of ignition timing is to make sure that each spark plug fires at exactly the right microsecond. How does this happen? Fortunately, there's an indicator on many engines that tells you exactly when a specific cylinder (usually #1) is ready for the spark. This indicator is mounted on the front of the car's engine. It's the crankshaft pulley that rotates as the engine does. When a mark on the rotating pulley is aligned with a mark on the stationary engine block, the ignition is in time.

The first question that might come to mind now is, "How do I know when those two marks are aligned?" The engine is running so fast. Here's how. Attach a tool called a timing light to the spark plug wire on the #1 or reference cylinder. The light will go on each time an electrical current is sent to that cylinder's spark plug. Point the timing light at the engine's timing mark and it will light up to show you the relationship between the mark and the reference point. Pretty snazzy, eh?

The other question you probably have is, "What do I do if the timing is off?" You adjust it by rotating the distributor slightly. A bolthead below the distributor, where it attaches to the engine block, can be loosened to allow the distributor to be turned, and then tightened when the timing is correct.

To adjust the ignition timing on your car, follow these steps:

1. Before starting the engine, use chalk or paint to identify the timing marks on the crankshaft pulley and the stationary pointer. Mark the scale as indicated by specifications. The manual or a plate or sticker on the car tells you where the mark should be. TDC means top dead center. BTDC means before top dead center and 5° BTDC means five degrees before top dead center.

2. Connect the timing light to the engine following the manufacturer's instructions. For most models, this means attaching the black lead wire to the negative terminal on the battery, attaching the red lead to the positive terminal, and attaching the third lead on or around the reference spark plug wire.

3. Loosen the adjustment nut or bolthead on the distributor base so that the distributor can be rotated to

adjust the timing. Be careful not to move the distributor yet.

4. If your car's manual says so, disconnect and plug the vacuum advance on the distributor. The vacuum advance (on older cars) uses increasing vacuum pressure to advance the timing at higher engine speeds. You don't want this to happen because it will throw off your ignition timing test, so disconnect the vacuum line and plug the hole with tape or a golf tee for now.

5. Make sure that all the timing light wires and other tools are clear of the fan blades before starting the engine. Start the engine and let it warm up for about 15 minutes. If the engine is running at a high idle speed, press the accelerator a couple of times to bring the engine down to normal idling speed.

6. Point the timing light at the ignition timing mark on the crankshaft pulley. If the marks are lined up, tighten the adjustment bolt on the base of the distributor. If they are not lined up, slowly rotate the distributor with your hand until the timing marks on the pulley are lined up and then tighten the adjustment bolt. If no amount of adjustment aligns the marks, or if aligning them makes the engine run very rough, you might not be using the correct spark plug wire. Stop, check everything for accuracy, and then start over.

7. After the distributor adjustment nut or bolthead is tightened, recheck the timing to make sure that nothing was moved in the process. If everything is okay, reinstall the vacuum advance (if any), and then remove the timing light connections.

8. Take your car for a test drive, stopping off for a milkshake or other frozen artificial dairy product.

Replace Engine Drive Belts (H)

The rotation of your car's engine not only rotates tires—it also powers the radiator cooling fan, the alternator, the air conditioning compressor, and the power steering (if any). That's efficient! The power is transferred from the engine to these components through drive belts. The belts wrap around the crankshaft pulley (introduced in the last adjustment) and pulley wheels for these other parts. Rubberized belts are used rather than chains because they are more pliable—and less expensive.

If the belts are too tight around the pulleys, the belts are stretched and they break. If they are too loose, the belts don't efficiently transfer power to the driven pulley. So your job, should you decide to accept it, is to make sure that the drive belts are adjusted properly. Which drive belts? Your car's service manual is more specific. Don't lose any sleep. Check them every six months or so and you'll be fine.

To check and replace the engine drive belts in most cars, follow these steps:

1. With the engine off, open the hood of the car and find the radiator and cooling fan. Behind the fan will be one or more drive belts wrapped around one or more grooved wheels called pulleys.

2. Visually inspect each drive belt for tears, small cracks, grease, and other signs of wear or damage. Especially inspect the inside of the drive belts—the part that fits into the pulley grooves—because this is the side that gets the most wear. Replace worn drive belts with ones of the same size, shape, and function. Some drive belts have the manufacturer's name and part number stamped on the outside edge of the belt. If not, a parts dealer can help you identify the exact replacement part.

3. To install a drive belt, first find the adjustment bolt. Loosen the adjustment bolt to allow movement of the driven pulley. Some drive belts have an automatic tensioner that also must be loosened. Remove the old drive belt and replace it with the new one. Use a prybar to move the driven pulley back to near where it was with the old belt and then tighten the adjustment bolt. Adjust the drive belt tension (unless done so by the automatic tensioner).

4. To adjust the drive belt tension, press against the outside of the belt about halfway between two pulleys. The movement of the drive belt is called the deflection. Typical deflection is about $1/4$ inch for drive belt spans (between pulleys) of less than 12 inches and about $1/2$ inch for spans of 12 to 18 inches. Loosen the adjustment bolt, use a prybar to move the driven pulley until the belt has the correct deflection, and then tighten the adjustment bolt.

Replace Chassis Lubricant (U)

There are many moving parts on your car. The engine, transmission/transaxle, and differential all have their own lubrication systems. Everything else that needs lubrication gets it under the category of chassis lubrication. The chassis includes the frame and secondary systems of your car: suspension, steering, and braking. These need lubrication to minimize wear.

Does your car's chassis need lubrication? Probably. Depending on the design of your car, some or all of the lubrication may be done for you by the manufacturer. Many newer cars are designed with sealed lubrication points. Others only need lubrication on a couple of parts every 12,000, 24,000, or more miles. Older cars require chassis lubrication as frequently as every 3,000 miles and at as many as 25 places on the car. Your car's owner's manual or service manual includes specific recommendations on chassis lubrication.

To replace the chassis lubricant in the typical, garden-variety car, follow these steps:

1. Gather the tools you'll need: wrenches, lubricating spray, and a grease gun. A grease gun, available at auto parts stores for about $10, forces thick lubricating grease into a fitting on your car when you squeeze the gun's handle.

2. Find the lubrication fittings on your car. A lube chart or service manual for your car shows you where they are. Most of them are on or around the steering linkage and the suspension system between the front wheels.

3. Lubricate the steering and suspension parts as needed. Some parts have a nipple, called a zerk fitting, on which you press the end of the grease gun. Other lubrication points have a small plug that must be screwed off to reveal the lubrication point.

Car Speak

Cars have moving joints just like you do. Instead of elbows and knees, they're called *universal* or *constant velocity (CV) joints*. Cars with straight drive-lines (rear-wheel drives) use universal joints. Cars with angled drivelines (front-wheel drives) use CV joints. Both types need chassis lubrication.

4. Make sure that you lubricate the miscellaneous chassis components as needed. They include the emergency or parking brake linkage, the transmission

shift linkage, and universal or CV joints. These are lubricated either with a grease gun or by smearing grease on friction points with your finger. Many cars also require a drop of light oil on some parts. Make sure that you hit the right part; oil is a conductor that can short out electrical components that are accidentally doused.

Chapter 7

Every-Two-Years Car Care: It's That Time Again, Again

In This Chapter

➤ How to safely and easily replace radiator coolant, cap, and hoses

➤ Replacing fuel and air filters in just a few minutes every couple of years

➤ How to replace spark plugs, plug wires, and other ignition parts using basic tools

➤ Replacing your car's transmission lubricants without getting too dirty in the process

Cars are getting smarter and smarter. Just a couple of decades ago, cars required more frequent servicing to keep them in good running condition. Ignition systems were tuned up every six months to a year. Fuel and air filters were replaced as often. On the other side of the issue, emission-control devices were simple. Today's cars are more complex and need less frequent service. It's a trade-off.

Whether your car is two or 25 years old, there are parts and fluids that need replacement. You can do that, as you'll learn in this chapter. These parts include some filters, spark plugs, ignition wiring and parts, and emission-control components. Fluids include transmission lubricants. Even if you don't replace them yourself, you can learn more about what they are and how to make sure you get your money's worth from someone who does replace them.

It's quiz time! What does the acronym H-U-B stand for in this book? Give up? H means under the hood, U designates adjustments done under the car, and B notes adjustments made beside the car.

So grab your car care toolbox (Chapter 2) and let's get torquing. I'll let you know what tools are needed as we go along.

Replace Radiator Coolant, Cap, and Hoses (H)

Your car's radiator uses more than just water to keep your engine from overheating. It uses a mixture of water and antifreeze fluid, also known as coolant. An anti-rust ingredient in the antifreeze works like the dickens to minimize the rust that is a byproduct of contact between water, air, and some metals. It's not totally successful. So every year or two, you should remove and replace the rust-laden coolant in your car's radiator.

At the same time, consider replacing the radiator cap and hoses on your car. These components also break down with use and can fail when you most need them.

To replace the radiator coolant, cap, and hoses in a typical car, follow these steps:

1. Remove the radiator cap and drain coolant from the cooling system. On most cars, this means placing a two- to five-gallon open container under the radiator and opening the drain fitting or removing the lower hose on the radiator. Some engines also have one or two coolant drain plugs on the engine block that must be removed to drain coolant from the block. Drain the coolant reservoir if possible. Your car's heater also may have a drain plug. In each case, make sure that you have a container to capture the draining coolant.

2. Flush the radiator system using fresh water and a radiator cleaner. You can purchase a radiator flush system at most auto parts retailers. It includes a cleaner as well as a plastic T-fitting that you install in a system hose. You then attach a garden hose to circulate fresh water through the system under pressure. Be sure to follow manufacturer's instructions if they contradict mine.

3. Check the condition of the radiator hoses by squeezing them. Replace them if they are soft or have cuts in them. In fact, it's relatively cheap insurance to replace the hoses as you replace the coolant. Hoses usually cost less when replacing them isn't an emergency. Inspect and, if necessary, replace the hose clamps at the same time.

4. Replace the coolant. Recommended coolant is half water and half antifreeze fluid available from auto parts retailers. Make sure that all drain plugs are tightened or replaced. Before adding the coolant to the radiator or reservoir, first open the car's heater temperature control to the maximum heat position so that the coolant also fills the heater core.

5. When you think the radiator or reservoir is full of coolant, start the car and let it warm up with the radiator cap off. The water pump inside the engine circulates the coolant, forcing air out of the system. When the upper radiator hose is warm to the touch, turn off the engine and let it cool. Then add more coolant as needed to fill the radiator or reservoir.

6. Replace the radiator pressure cap with a new one.

7. Start the engine again and let it warm up. As it does, inspect the radiator, reservoir, hoses, engine block drain plugs, and heater core for leaks. If you find leaks, refer to Chapter 11, or take your car to a radiator shop for repairs.

8. Properly dispose of the old coolant (not down a storm drain!). Seal it in a plastic container and take it to your local recycling center for disposal. Most coolants are both sweet and poisonous to pets, so clean up any spills.

Replace Fuel Filter (H)

Gasoline is processed petroleum. During the processing, contaminants are removed. However, gas then is stored in imperfect tanks with rust and bits of metal or plastic. The worst culprit is your own car's gas tank, where contaminants can build up on the bottom. If the engine is operated when the tank is almost empty, these contaminants can be pumped to your engine along with the gas. They then can enter the carburetor or fuel injectors and block operation.

Fortunately, today's cars have filters in the fuel line to stop the big chunks from entering the carburetor or fuel injectors. Even older cars (like my 40-plus-year-old Continental) have been retrofitted with fuel filters to minimize big chunks in the carburetors. Replacing the fuel filter on most cars is a piece of cake.

To replace the fuel filter on your car, follow these steps:

1. Find the fuel filter. First, check your car's owner's manual or service manual for the location. On some cars, it's under the hood—a small aluminum barrel in the fuel line between the fuel pump and the carburetor. On other cars, it's a plastic-cased filter installed on the carburetor, near the fuel-injection unit, or on the fuel pump. Some are installed near the fuel tank. A few cars have two fuel filters—one near the tank and one near the carburetor.

2. Remove the fuel filter. In-line fuel filters can be removed by hand by carefully loosening clamps at each end of the filter unit and then pulling the fuel lines off the filter. Fuel filters installed on the carburetor or fuel pump require that you use a wrench to first loosen the fuel line and then remove the filter.

Mechanic's Tip

Fuel-injection systems pressurize fuel to deliver it to the engine. To replace the fuel filter on a fuel-injection system, you first must relieve system pressure. Refer to the car's service manual for specific information on how to do so safely.

3. Replace the fuel filter. You can find a replacement fuel filter at your favorite auto parts store or many hardware stores. There probably will be a brand name and a parts number on the filter. If not, an auto parts salesperson or a reference book can tell you which filter you need. Also make sure that the clamps or fittings on the filter are in good shape, replacing them as needed.

Replace Air Filter (H)

Air isn't what it used to be. A car's air filter can tell you this. Look at a used air filter and you can see a broad collection of stuff your car otherwise would have breathed. The history of air filters also illustrates the growth of pollution and a car's need for clean air. Early cars had no air filter. Later cars had an oil-bath filter system that caught bugs and bits before they were sucked up by the carburetor. Today's cars have large and fairly efficient filters to keep most objects out of the carburetor or fuel-injection system. (Wouldn't it be great if we all had replaceable air filters in us?)

Fuel-injection systems are especially sensitive to clogged air filters. Although a clogged filter won't damage your car, it can dramatically reduce power. And a new air filter probably will cost you less than $10. Replacing your car's air filter is one of the easier tasks you can do for your car's health. Some folks do it every year. Here's how.

To replace the air filter in your highly-financed car, follow these steps:

1. Find the air filter. For carbureted cars, the air filter usually is located above the carburetor in a large round object euphemistically called the air cleaner. For fuel-injected cars, the filter is located in a large hose somewhere between the car's front grill and the engine.

2. Remove the air filter. For carbureted cars, remove the wingnut on top of the air cleaner and lift off the top to expose the round air filter. For fuel-injected cars, remove the clips or twistnuts on the filter cover and lift the air filter from the unit, noting which way it came out so that you can put the new one back in the same way. Use an old rag to wipe out the

air cleaner, discarding any waylaid bugs or other foreign objects. (I found a live salamander in one of my car's air cleaners! Honest!)

3. Replace the air filter. Place the new air filter against the old one to make sure that it is the same size. This also tells you something about the amount of contaminants your air filter stopped since it was last replaced. Install the new air filter in the same way that the old one was installed. Some paper filters are wrapped with a foam blanket that initially filters bugs and other large projectiles. Filters for fuel-injection systems usually go in only one way, whereas those for carbureted systems can go in correctly with either side up. Make sure that the filter sits well and isn't lopsided.

4. Replace other parts you took off to get to the filter.

Many cars have an air cleaner that controls the source of air going through the filter and to the carburetor or injection system. It pulls warmer air from the exhaust manifold when the engine is cold and from the outside air when the engine warms up. As you are working around the air cleaner, make sure that the air duct from the engine is securely in place. Visually inspect the air cleaner housing and regulator for disconnections and damage.

Replace Spark Plugs (H)

Spark plugs are an important part of your car's engine. They supply the fire that ignites the controlled explosions within each cylinder.

Today's cars are sufficiently efficient that the spark plugs only need replacement every couple of years or about 25,000 miles. Unfortunately, car manufacturers have used this fact to make spark plugs less accessible than they were on earlier engines. In fact, on some engines, it is a chore just finding all the spark plugs, let alone trying to replace them. After you find them, you might decide to replace them yourself or to hire a dexterous mechanic for the job.

To find the spark plugs, first find the car's distributor or ignition computer. It will have four to eight wires running from it. Follow each of these wires and you will, hopefully, find the spark plugs. Optionally, check your car's owner's manual or service manual for a drawing of the engine that may indicate where the spark plugs are hidden.

To replace the spark plugs in your car, follow these steps:

1. Purchase your spark plugs. Auto parts retailers can supply replacement spark plugs. However, a previous owner or mechanic might have installed spark plugs that operate at hotter or colder temperatures, so you might want to remove and check the brand and number on the plug before buying a set. Be careful of what you install because a spark plug that is too long can damage the engine's internal parts. Your best bet is to use the spark plug recommended by the manufacturer. How many? One for each cylinder: four for a four-cylinder engine, six for a six-cylinder engine, and eight spark plugs for an eight-cylinder engine.

2. Set the gap for all the spark plugs. Spark plugs supply electrical spark to the cylinder by making it jump a small gap at the end of the plug. The gap between the center electrode and ground electrode must be exactly as recommended by the manufacturer. Use a gap gauge (a couple of dollars at the auto parts store) to set the gap between the electrodes. If the gap isn't correct, you can carefully bend the ground or wire electrode until it is.

3. Remove the old plug. First, make sure that your engine hasn't been run within an hour or more so that

you don't burn yourself on hot engine parts. After you find the spark plug, grasp the spark plug wire where it attaches to the spark plug end or terminal and carefully pull it off. Depending on how easy the spark plugs are to reach, you may need to use a spark plug wire puller (less than $10 at you-know-where). Then use an old paint brush to sweep away any dirt and debris from around the spark plugs. You don't want that stuff falling into the cylinder hole when the spark plug is removed. Use a spark plug wrench to grasp and turn the spark plug counterclockwise to remove it. This may require some force.

4. Install the new (gapped) plug. If you can easily reach it by hand, place the end of the spark plug in the cylinder hole and screw it in. If you can't quite reach it, push a 6- to 12-inch length of 3/8-inch hose on the terminal to extend your reach. Don't force the spark plug into the hole or you will ruin the threads on the side of the plug. Tighten the spark plug into the hole using a torque wrench or a standard spark plug wrench. Overtightening can break the plug and add time and frustration to the job.

5. Reinstall the spark plug wire.

6. Repeat the process for the other spark plugs.

You can learn much about the operation of your car's engine by inspecting the old spark plugs. A service manual or an auto parts store will have a chart showing what spark plugs may look like and what caused the problem: overheating, carbon, oil, poor fuel, preignition, and so on. Don't be afraid to ask a knowledgeable clerk to help you interpret what the plugs are telling you.

Replace Spark Plug Wires (H)

Hold it! Time for a seventh-inning stretch. Harry Carey isn't available to sing "Take Me Out to the Ballgame," but feel free to hum it. Okay. We're back now.

Today's wires use a carbon or silicon conductor that is sensitive to mishandling and to age. I know *that* feeling! Many car manufacturers now recommend that the spark plug wires be replaced when the spark plugs are replaced.

To replace the spark plug wires in your car, follow these steps:

1. Purchase a replacement set of spark plug wires for your car as recommended by the manufacturer. A replacement set will have wires cut to the correct lengths and include contacts and boots for each end. Some sets also will have numbers on the wires to help you identify the cylinder to which they go.

2. Find the spark plug wires on your car. To do so, find the car's distributor or ignition computer. Wires will lead from it to the spark plugs. The wires may feed through one or more brackets, called looms, that isolate the wires from the maze of other wires and hoses under the hood. You also may need to replace the looms, depending on how easy the wires are to remove from the looms. Some spark plug wire sets come with new looms or replacement bridges.

3. Replace the wires, one at a time. Select one spark plug wire and trace it from the computer or distributor to the spark plug. Then select the replacement spark plug wire of the same length. Follow the instructions that came with the wire set on how to install it on your car. If it feeds through a hole in a loom, you may need to remove a boot from one end to do so.

4. Repeat the process for each spark plug wire until all are installed. Recheck both ends of each wire to ensure that they fit snugly.

Replace Other Ignition Parts (H)

Depending on what type of ignition system your car uses, there will be other parts that need replacement. Older cars have breaker-point ignitions. Newer ones have breakerless ignitions. The newest cars have computerized ignitions. You can replace some of these parts, but you may not want to or be able to replace ignition parts on newer cars.

To replace other ignition parts in your car, follow these steps:

1. Identify what type of ignition system your car has and what it needs. The car's service manual will tell you and also identify the parts to be replaced. Breaker-point distributors need new contact points, a condenser, a rotor, and a cap. Breakerless ignition systems need a new rotor and cap, and sometimes one or two other components. A computerized ignition may not need anything. To find out what your car needs, identify your car to an auto parts counterperson.

2. Disassemble the ignition and replace parts as described in the car's service manual. For many cars, this means first removing the distributor cap. The distributor cap is the round plastic part that gathers the ends of all the spark plug wires.

3. To replace the cap, first align the old and new caps side-by-side with the notch underneath both caps at the same relative position. Then remove one spark plug wire from the old cap and place it at the same position on the new cap. One-by-one, repeat this process for all spark plug wires as well as the coil wire that fits in the center of the cap.

4. To replace the distributor rotor, first remove the distributor cap. Then lift the old rotor from the center of the distributor. Visually check to make sure that the new rotor is the same size and shape as the old one. The hole on the underside of the new rotor will have a notch that shows how it fits on the distributor shaft key. Install it by matching the notch and the key.

5. To replace contact points and the condenser on a breaker-point distributor, follow the car manufacturer's recommendations as offered in the service manual. In most cases, the engine is rotated until the corners of the distributor shaft push the contact points open to a specific gap. Replace the old contact points with a new set and adjust the gap. Replace the condenser (this stores electricity between sparks).

6. To replace parts in a breakerless distributor or a computerized ignition, follow the manufacturer's recommendations. There are just too many variations to cover in this book.

Replace PCV, EEC, and EGR Parts (H, U)

It's acronym time! In an attempt to reduce emissions from our cars, engineers and bureaucrats have worked overtime developing long names for simple devices. Here are a few:

➤ EEC: Evaporative emissions canister

➤ EGR: Exhaust gas recirculation

➤ PCV: Positive crankcase ventilation

➤ RGDFMYCUC: Rube Goldberg device for making your car unnecessarily complicated

Fortunately, replacing parts for these systems is not always as complicated. In fact, many cars have a road map to their emissions-control systems affixed to the inside of the car's hood.

To replace emissions-control system parts on your car, follow these steps:

1. Find the diagram of your car's emissions-control system. It may be under the hood, on the engine compartment firewall, or in the car's service manual. From this map, identify which parts need periodic replacement and when. They usually are marked.

2. Purchase the replacement part from your auto parts supplier (dealer or retailer). Ask the parts salesperson for directions or suggestions on installing the part. If the response is "Huh?", find another parts source.

3. Replace the part. In most cases, installation is straightforward: Remove the clips holding the part in place, remove the old part, install the new part, and replace the clips. Fortunately, parts that are intended to be replaced on a regular basis often are designed to be replaced easily. EGR units are mounted on the intake or exhaust manifold. PCV valves are usually mounted on the engine's valve cover. EECs are often located near the front of the engine compartment, identified by two or more hoses.

Replace Automatic Transmission Filter and Fluid (U)

Automatic transmissions are made to be trouble-free for 100,000 miles or more. They don't last that long if they don't get maintenance every year or two. What maintenance? Replacing the fluid and filter.

To replace the automatic transmission filter and fluid in the typical car, follow these steps:

1. Purchase the correct filter and fluid designed for your car's automatic transmission (Chapter 3). Depending on the transmission, you also may need a gasket. Don't buy cheap. Buy quality for a couple dollars more. Also find an open container, such as an oil change drip pan, for collecting the old automatic transmission fluid. Place the pan under the automatic transmission.

2. Safely jack up your car and place stands under it so that you have room to work. Gather your tools: screwdrivers or wrenches for removing the transmission plug or pan.

3. Remove the transmission plug or pan. Some automatic transmissions have a drain plug just like the one on the engine's oil pan. Other transmissions don't have such a plug so the pan must be carefully removed to drain the fluid. Here's how: Loosen the bolts attaching the pan to the front of the transmission three or four turns, but don't remove them. Then carefully loosen and remove the bolts attaching the rest of the pan to the transmission. Be careful because, once tipped, the fluid in the pan will begin draining over the edge. The fluid might be hot.

4. After the fluid is drained, carefully remove the pan to expose the transmission fluid filter. Remove the filter and replace it with a new one following the manufacturer's instructions.

5. Clean the transmission pan with a rag, replace the gasket if needed, and reinstall the pan. Reinstall the drain plug if there is one. Remove the car from the safety stands.

6. Refill the transmission with the recommended automatic transmission fluid, using a funnel to pour it into the transmission dipstick tube. How much? Check your car's owner's manual or service manual for specifics. Three to six quarts is typical.

7. Start the engine and let it warm up. Make sure that the brake is set. Slowly move the transmission through the gear selector a few times to circulate the fluid through the automatic transmission. Then stop the engine and recheck the fluid level using the automatic transmission dipstick. Add as needed.

8. Take your car for a test ride. Junk-food stop is optional, but recommended.

Replace Manual Transmission/Transaxle Lubricant (U)

This one isn't required, but it's smart motoring. Your car's manual may not suggest replacing the manual transmission lubricant. It makes sense to do so, however, just as you would replace any other lubricant that comes in contact with moving parts.

To replace the manual transmission/transaxle lubricant in your car, follow these steps:

1. Safely jack up your car and place stands underneath to give yourself a safe and spacious work area. You'll probably only need a wrench and a drain pan for this job.

2. Find the drain plug at the lowest point on one side of the manual transmission. Place the drain pan under it to catch the two to four quarts of lubricant that will drain from it. Use a wrench to turn the drain plug counterclockwise and remove the plug. After gravity has done its job, replace the drain plug.

3. Find the fill/level plug located above the drain plug on the side of the manual transmission. Remove the fill/level plug as you did the drain plug. Following the manufacturer's recommendations, fill the manual transmission with lubricant until it begins to flow out of the fill hole. Verify that the level is at the bottom of the hole with your pinky finger. Depending on available space and the size of the lubricant's container, you might need to use a suction tool to get the lubricant into the hole. There's not much room to move an oil can into position on some cars. Insert the tip of the suction tool's hose into the lubricant's container and pull on the plunger, drawing lubricant up into the tool's storage chamber. Then place the tool's hose tip into the fill hole and press on the plunger, forcing the lubricant into the tranny (the familiar version of transmission). It's actually kind of fun, albeit sloppy. But it makes some pretty rude noises.

4. Replace the fill/level plug, making sure that it is tight.

Chapter 8

What's Wrong with Your Car: Diagnostics for the Clueless

In This Chapter
- ➤ Performing an easy diagnostics test that the mechanic would charge you for
- ➤ Listening to tell-tale noises
- ➤ Troubleshooting by the book
- ➤ Ya gonna fix it or what?

No, troubleshooting doesn't mean shooting your car if it gives you trouble!

Troubleshooting means finding and fixing the source of car trouble. You don't necessarily have to fix the problem yourself—you can hire someone to do it. But you do need to know what the problem is. Why? So that you can say,

"Try that again?!" when the mechanic says, "A million dollars for a new muffler bearing."

This chapter offers a number of proven tips for trouble-shooting your car and getting it repaired at a reasonable cost. The remainder of this book describes how specific repairs are done on unspecific cars.

The Professional Mechanic's Three-Minute Diagnostic Test

How do professional mechanics diagnose a car in just a few minutes? They use their common sense: They look for signs, listen for noises, and feel for problems. Knowing what a car should look and sound like, they easily recognize what shouldn't be. You can do the same thing; as you drive or perform routine maintenance, look, listen, and feel.

That's what your doctor probably does—uses common sense to find symptoms—before he or she tries to diagnose a problem. How are you feeling today? Where does it hurt? Does it hurt when I do this? Visa or MasterCard?

Learn and use these diagnostic techniques even if you have no desire to lift a wrench in repair. Why? Because you'll be better able to describe the symptoms to your mechanic. Mechanics are people, too—with some notable exceptions. If you tell a mechanic that the valves need to be adjusted, that's what will be done—even if the problem is simply a loose wire. So don't tell your mechanic what's wrong; tell the mechanic the car's specific symptoms.

How can you clearly describe the symptoms?

➤ **Describe what the problem looks, sounds, or feels like:**

The muffler looks like it's red hot.

The engine sounds like marbles are rolling around inside.

The air from the heater feels moist.

➤ **Describe where in the car the problem occurs:**

The glow looks like it's emanating from behind the glove compartment.

The noise sounds like it's coming from the area around the right-rear wheel.

The wobble feels like it's in the rear half of the car.

➤ **Describe when the problem happens:**

The front-left tire is low after it's parked overnight.

The car feels like it pulls to the right when I step hard on the brakes.

The engine sounds rough when I drive it at over 120 mph.

Your Noisy Car and What It's Telling You

So what kinds of noises might you hear as you merrily roll along?

➤ Clicking

➤ Squealing

➤ Growling

➤ Whistling

➤ Thumping

➤ Humming

➤ Chirping

➤ Rattling

➤ Knocking

Knowing the type, location, and time of the sound often can help you pinpoint the problem. A growling sound from below the middle of the back seat when the car is moving probably is caused by a problem in the differential (on a rear-wheel drive car), for example. If you hear a sound when accelerating like a bunch of marbles banging around in the engine, the problem probably is preignition caused by low octane fuel or incorrect engine timing.

Knowing what you now know about cars, you might be able to identify the source of the problem. If not, you can save money by accurately describing the sound, its source, and when you hear it to your mechanic.

How about smells? What kinds of unusual odors emanate from a vehicle that operates on gas?

➤ Burning oil

➤ Burning plastic

➤ Burning fabric

➤ Burning putridity

The smell of burning oil can be something as simple as oil spilled on the engine's exhaust manifold or as serious as the engine's piston rings failing. The smell of burning plastic can mean a problem with the electrical wiring or interior parts. Odors like burning day at the city dump are either that or the catalytic converter failing.

To troubleshoot smells, first stop the car as soon and as safely as possible, and then turn off the ignition. Get out and walk around the car, sniffing to identify the location of the odor. After you identify the odor, you can decide whether it's safe to go on or whether you should call for a tow truck.

> **Dollar Saver**
>
> You can listen to your car using a homemade stethoscope. Attach a piece of rubber vacuum hose to the end of a metal rod. Holding the rubber end to your ear, carefully place the metal tip against the running engine until you've identified the noise's source. Don't touch electrical wires, hot parts, or fan blades. Your car's service manual can help you identify the culprit.

The Idiot's Warning System

How can you be sure that your car's gauges are telling you the truth? Experience. Yes, you can test them. But driving your car gives you the experience to know which readings are normal and which aren't. Gauges report trends.

How can you be sure that your car's warning lights are equally honest? Warning lights report status. You can make sure that your warning lights work by watching the dashboard as you turn on the ignition. Most modern cars light all warning devices then to let you know that the bulbs work. Your car's owner's manual will tell you what the lights mean and whether they are tested as the ignition switch is moved.

The point here is this: Whether you are dealing with gauges or lights, learn to read them. Make a habit of scanning your car's dashboard on a regular basis. When starting your car, turn the ignition switch to the ON position and watch the gauges and/or lights. With gauges, know what's normal. If necessary, apply a piece of tape on gauges to clearly identify normal operating ranges (some gauges are as useless as warning lights).

Troubleshooting by the Book

The lone figure in this chapter provides a useful trouble-shooting guide to help you find later chapters in this book to help you solve common automotive problems (or at least to help diagnose what's going on). Begin in the upper left-hand corner of the flow chart, and answer the questions down the left-hand side. When you get to a question you answer "no" to, look to the right to learn which chapter in this book offers more information about your car's problems. For example, if your car doesn't start OK, read Chapter 9 for troubleshooting tips and repair techniques.

For precise help, most service manuals include a trouble-shooting guide that covers a specific make and model of car. Not only are such guides more accurate to your car's symptoms, but they typically are cross-referenced to the solution.

Ya Gonna Fix It or What?

Okay, you've identified the problem. Is the solution to replace a part or to repair it? With all the firmness I can muster, I respond: That depends.

Repairing many car components requires tools you probably don't have or want. Why buy a $2,000 tool to fix a $50 part? Okay, maybe you won Lotto America! Otherwise, don't bother. The total cost of starter parts, for example, is greater than the cost of a rebuilt starter—as long as you give them your old starter in exchange so that it can be rebuilt. The same goes for engines, transmissions, and many other parts: Buy and replace them as a unit, making sure the new parts are the same model numbers as the old ones. In fact, engine and transmission rebuilding are really too much for must folks to tackle—so this book doesn't. (In fact, when my Continental recently needed the tired engine rebuilt, I hired a professional mechanic to do the job. I'm not an idiot, ya know!)

How long will the repair take? Available through larger libraries, a flat-rate manual estimates the amount of time required by a trained mechanic to perform defined jobs on specific cars. By doubling the time, you probably can estimate how long it will take an untrained owner to do the same job—maybe more, maybe less.

Troubleshooting Guide

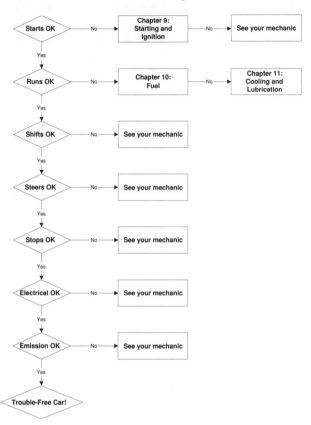

Chapter 9

Electrical System Repairs: Finding the Spark in Your Ride

In This Chapter

➤ How to safely test and replace a car battery and cables

➤ Installing a new alternator

➤ Checking out and replacing other components in your car's electrical system

➤ Diagnosing starter and ignition problems with common sense

➤ How to replace a defective starter without getting too dirty

➤ Repairing common ignition system problems that keep you from going anywhere

Your car both produces and consumes power. Part of the engine's power is used to produce electrical power, which then is consumed by the computers, spark plugs, lights, radio, and other paraphernalia. The battery is the power storage room.

Your car's charging system includes the alternator, voltage regulator, battery, cables, wires, and fuses.

The ignition system is your car's nervous system.

The starting system then must be the first cup of coffee in the morning. And we all know what some people are like if they don't get their coffee fix!

This chapter guides you through common repairs to electrical, charging, starting, and ignition systems. Reading over the instructions can help you decide whether you want to tackle the project yourself or to hire someone to do it. Remember that, although you don't know as much about your car as a trained mechanic, you have a greater need to make sure that the job is done right and at a reasonable cost. You're the boss.

If troubleshooting (see Chapter 8 or your car's service manual) says you need to repair electrical components, here's how. Most components in your car's automotive electrical systems are replaced rather than repaired. In fact, they are a commodity item. You can find them on the shelf of most auto parts stores or through mail-order suppliers and replace them yourself.

Dollar Saver

Fuses first! Whenever anything in your car's electrical system goes out, find the fuse box (identified in the car's owner's manual) and look for a blown fuse. Some fuse boxes are under the hood near the battery. Others are under the dashboard near the driver. Some cars have fuses in both locations. A blown fuse will have a visible break in the wire that runs through it.

Troubleshooting Tips for the Electrically Dysfunctional

I know you've been waiting anxiously for these. Here are a few useful tips for troubleshooting electrical and charging systems.

➤ If the battery tests OK but won't hold a charge, make sure that the alternator drive belt is adjusted tight. If the drive belt is OK, test the voltage regulator using a volt-ohmmeter.

➤ If turn signals work only on one side, check the bulb and wiring on the side that isn't working. If the bulb and wiring don't work at all, check the fuse.

➤ If you suspect that your car's battery is weak, pull your car up to a garage door or other wall and turn the headlights on for a moment. If they are bright, the battery and voltage regulator are OK. If they are dim but brighten after the engine has been started, the battery is bad. If they are bright but the engine turns slowly when started, the starter is bad (covered later in this chapter).

Energize Me!

A car battery is an electrical storage device. It receives electricity from the alternator/regulator and passes it on to other electrical components on demand. As the battery's electricity is used up, it is replaced by the alternator. Problems occur when a battery isn't strong enough to keep a charge because the electrolyte is weak. This typically occurs a few days after the warranty expires.

To safely jump a dead battery using another vehicle's battery, follow these steps:

1. Use a jumper cable to connect the dead battery's positive terminal to the helper car's positive terminal.

2. Connect the helper car's negative terminal to a bolthead on the disabled car's engine.

3. Start the helper car's engine, and then start the disabled car's engine.

4. After the car that had the dead battery starts, remove the jumper cable in the reverse order of how it was installed.

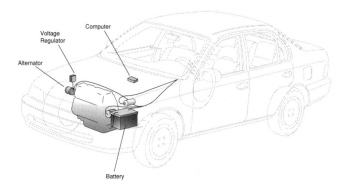

An automotive charging system.

To replace a battery, follow these steps:

1. Find your car's battery. It is usually under the hood and typically on the passenger's side of the car.

2. Disconnect the cable from the negative side of the battery first and then from the positive side.

3. Remove the hold-down clamp or frame that keeps the battery in place. Typically, this means removing nuts from the end of two long bolts. Grasp the bolts as you loosen the nuts, making sure that the released bolts don't fall out of reach.

Dollar Saver

A more expensive battery can be worth the extra expense. A 60-month battery is built to hold a charge longer than a 48-month battery. So is a 60-month battery worth the extra money? Yes, it is—if you plan on keeping your car that long. If you plan to sell your car in the next year, a 36- or 48-month battery will do just fine and cost less.

4. Use a battery strap (from the auto parts store) attached to the two terminals to lift and remove the HEAVY battery. Set it aside for a moment.

5. Inspect the battery tray for corrosion and damage. If the tray is rusted or damaged, replace it. Using rubber gloves, clean the battery with baking soda and water to neutralize the battery acids.

6. Test the battery or have it tested to make sure that it will hold a charge. If it will, recharge the battery or have it recharged by a mechanic. If it won't, replace the battery with one of the same voltage, size, amperage rating, and cold-cranking rating. Consider replacing the battery cables at the same time (see the following section, "Your Car's Battery Gets Cable").

7. Reinstall the battery, hold-down clamp, positive cable, and then negative cable.

8. Lift your right hand over your head, bend your elbow to 120°, and then move your wrist repeatedly, patting yourself on the back.

Your Car's Battery Gets Cable

The battery cables play a vital part in delivering electricity to and from the car's battery. Battery cables are simply heavy-duty coated wires with terminals on the ends to make attaching them to the battery and other components easier.

So what can go wrong with battery cables? They can become corroded by the electrochemical process that's going on inside the battery. Corrosion is a buildup of powdery substance on the cable ends. The ends can also be damaged by mishandling or become brittle with age.

To replace your battery cables, follow these steps:

1. Find your car's battery. It is under the hood and typically on the passenger's side of the car. There are two cables attached to two terminals on the top or side of the battery. One is probably red and the other is probably black.

2. Disconnect the cable from the negative side of the battery and then from the positive side. The negative cable is usually black and smaller than the red, positive cable.

3. Disconnect the cables at the other end. The negative ground cable (usually the black one) probably is connected to the engine. The positive cable (red) probably is connected to the starter solenoid.

4. Inspect the cable wire and ends for damage. Even if you can't see it, there may be damage to the wires within the cable, reducing the flow of electricity through it. Battery cables are just a few dollars each, so replace them every few years whether or not you can see damage. The easiest time to replace cables is when you replace the battery, every four or five years.

5. To find replacement cables, clean the old cables and take them to your favorite auto parts retailer for an exact match. You want the new ones to match the old ones in length, circumference, and ends. If you have a choice, spend a couple extra bucks and buy ones with better quality wires to transport electricity more easily. Cheap is cheap. Pick up some battery terminal corrosion inhibitor (or petroleum jelly) while you're at the store—and a candy bar for me.

6. Reinstall the ends of the cables to the ground and the starter solenoid or wherever they came from, applying corrosion inhibitor to the bolt threads.

7. Apply corrosion inhibitor to the positive battery terminal. Reinstall the positive (red) cable to the positive terminal on the battery.

8. Apply corrosion inhibitor to the negative battery terminal. Reinstall the negative (black) cable to the negative terminal on the battery.

No Charge? You've Been Replaced!

An alternator produces electricity from a car's engine. If your car's battery is in good condition, but isn't getting recharged, the charging system may be the culprit.

An alternator should give you at least 50,000 miles of service, and up to twice as much. Before you replace an alternator, check its drive belt and pulley to make sure they aren't the cause of the problem.

To test and replace an alternator, follow these steps:

1. To test the charging system's fuse, first locate the fuse by using the car's service manual. It may be a fuse box or it may be on the wire between the starter solenoid and the alternator. Make sure that the engine and ignition are off. Use an ohmmeter, placing

one probe on one side of the fuse or wire and one on the other. If the fuse or wire has infinite resistance (1), the circuit is open and the fuse should be replaced.

 Car Speak

Your car's *alternator* converts mechanical energy into alternating current (AC), which then must be changed (rectified) into direct current (DC) for use by the car's electrical system. Also known as an AC generator.

A *generator* is a device that converts mechanical energy into direct current (DC) for use by the car's electrical system. Also known as a DC generator.

---

2. To test the alternator, refer to the car's service manual for instructions on how to do so without removing the alternator from the car. One way of testing the system is by checking the battery's voltage with a volt-ohmmeter (VOM). With the engine off, the battery should give a reading of about 12 volts. With the engine on, the battery should give a reading of 14 to 15 volts on the VOM. If not, replace the alternator. If it is more than 15 volts, replace the voltage regulator.

3. To replace the alternator, first disconnect the cable from the negative terminal of the battery. Then identify and remove all wires from the alternator. Loosen the alternator adjusting bolt, and then remove the drive belt. Remove the alternator from the adjusting bracket and the engine. Replace the alternator with one of the exact same size and rating.

Mechanic's Tip

If you replace your alternator, make sure that the replacement has drive belt pulleys. If not (often not), remove them from the old alternator and install them on the new one before returning or recycling the old alternator.

More Power to You

The voltage regulator plays an important role in your car's charging system: It manages the alternator's output voltage.

How can you tell if the regulator isn't working as it should? By checking voltage of the battery with the engine running. If the battery voltage is less than 12 volts or more than 15 volts, the regulator is probably not working. Although you can replace the regulator without replacing the alternator, you should consider doing both at once.

Don't forget to disconnect the negative battery terminal when working on your car's electrical system. And be prepared to reenter alarm codes if necessary, after the battery cable is reattached.

To replace a voltage regulator, follow these steps:

1. Find the darn thing. Your car's service manual helps you locate it. Otherwise, older cars have the voltage regulator mounted on the firewall or a cowl (a wheel cover inside the engine compartment) and newer ones use a solid state regulator installed on the front side of the alternator behind the pulley wheel.

2. Loosen mounting screws and remove the regulator. Don't attempt to repair it. Replace it.

3. Take the regulator to your auto parts retailer along with model numbers from the alternator on which it was installed. Make sure that the replacement is the same size, shape, and rating as the unit it is replacing.

4. Install the voltage regulator, making sure that all wires are connected correctly.

5. When done, test the voltage regulator to make sure that it is working as it should.

How To Be an Automotive Electrician for Fun and Profit—Well, at Least Fun

There are many electrical devices within your car that sometimes can go awry. They include lights, instruments, controls, radio, clock, and wiring (see figure illustrating this system). Most devices have two wires; some have more. You easily can test these devices by checking the circuit to make sure that electricity has a closed path through it.

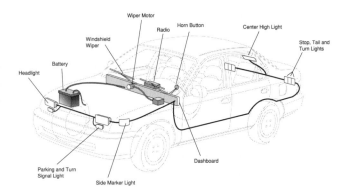

All the things that power brings.

Troubleshooting Electrical Problems

Here are some guidelines for troubleshooting starting and ignition systems:

➤ Make sure that the automatic transmission is in the Park (P) position or that the clutch on a manual transmission is fully depressed (or at least morose).

➤ If your car won't even make a noise when you try to start it, first check the battery terminal connections. Then look for other loose connections in the starting and ignition systems.

➤ If your car won't start, causes may be a discharged battery, loose or broken wires, a faulty starter or solenoid, or a faulty ignition switch or neutral interlock, mentioned earlier in this chapter.

➤ Dirty battery connections can cause fuel-injection systems to hesitate or surge. Keep those connections clean!

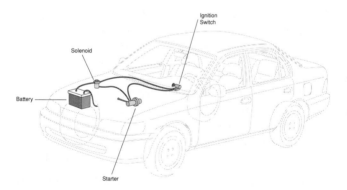

An automotive starting system.

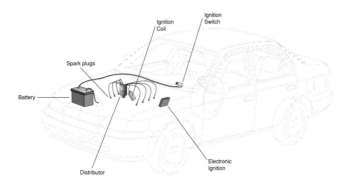

An automotive ignition system.

Some Days It's Hard to Get Started

The job of the starting system is to turn the engine quickly enough to enable it to start. Components of the starting system include the battery, the starter motor, the starter solenoid, and all the wires that connect these parts.

How does the starter system work? As you turn the ignition key to the start position, an electric signal runs along the wire to the starter solenoid. The solenoid is told to deliver electricity from the battery to the starter motor. It does so until the ignition key is released from the start position. The end of the starter motor has a small gear that meshes with the teeth around the edge of the engine flywheel. The gear rotates the flywheel. At the same time, the ignition system is delivering a spark and the fuel system is supplying fuel/air to the engine. The engine starts.

If the engine doesn't start, the cause could be one of many things, including the starter or solenoid. Before you consider repairing the starter, however, check one more thing: the interlock. An interlock stops something from happening if all conditions are not met. Most cars now have an interlock that must be operated before the signal to start is sent to the solenoid. The interlock on cars with manual transmissions requires that the clutch pedal be pushed in before the car is allowed to start. On automatic transmissions, the interlock requires that the gear selector be in the park or neutral position.

So, before you begin to repair your car's starter or solenoid, find and test the interlock, fuses, and battery. Finding the interlock may be the operative term here, because some are mounted near the clutch pedal, whereas others are in the steering column or mounted near the starter. Testing an interlock means using an ohmmeter to see whether the circuit is open or closed (read the ohmmeter's instructions) when it is activated.

One more tip before we get our hands dirty: Have someone turn the ignition key to the start position. If, standing near the engine, you hear the solenoid click, it's working. If you don't, it's not working, assuming that you've already checked the battery and any starter system fuses.

Starter Replacement for the Automotively Learned

To replace the starter motor and/or starter solenoid, follow these steps:

Mechanic's Tip
Before disconnecting the battery cables on cars with alarm systems, make sure that you have the manufacturer's code. Otherwise, your alarm system or radio won't work after you've reconnected the battery.

1. Remove the negative or ground cable from the battery.

2. Find the starter. It's a round motor about three inches across located at one side or the other of the flywheel. The flywheel is located between the engine and transmission. The solenoid probably is mounted on the side of the starter. If not, trace the wire to the solenoid, which probably is mounted nearby on the firewall.

3. Disconnect the battery cable and any other wires to the starter or solenoid.

4. Remove the starter and solenoid. This usually means removing two bolts that mount the starter on the side of the engine or the bellhousing (clutch cover). The starter weighs a few pounds, so be careful not to drop it when the last bolt is loosened. If the solenoid is not attached to the starter, remove it from the firewall.

5. Repair or replace the starter and solenoid. Unless you have the equipment and knowledge to repair or rebuild a starter (which I'm assuming you don't), buy a replacement at an auto parts store or automotive electrical shop. Either one should be able to test your starter and solenoid first before you buy a replacement.

6. Reinstall the starter and solenoid. Tighten and check all connections before trying to use the starter.

Solving Ignition Incontinence

An automotive ignition system has a pretty simple job: to supply a spark to the engine at the time it's most needed. To do so on today's fuel-efficient cars requires nothing short of a computer, however. That's why cars have become so difficult for the owner to repair. Fortunately, the technology has stabilized somewhat and the newest cars at least have some logic to them.

In addition, cars are using systems that are more modularized. No one, not even mechanics, repairs ignition systems. They replace components that test bad. So can you. Using a simple volt-ohmmeter (VOM) and the car's service manual, you probably can track down and solve many ignition system problems.

Getting Your Wires Straight

The ignition switch in a car used to be a simple, three-position switch: Off, On, and Start. Today, it's linked to sensors, anti-theft devices, interlocks, and the bank where you have your car loan.

Fortunately, failure of an ignition switch typically is traced to a loose wire. That's something you can fix—if you can find it.

To repair an ignition switch and wiring, follow these steps:

1. Find an electrical schematic for your car's ignition system. It may be printed in the car's service manual or in an aftermarket service manual. If not, you might have to order one through the dealer. The schematic tells you what's in the ignition wiring system, such as interlocks and sensors, besides the switch. It also may identify their locations. Or not!

2. Visually trace and inspect the ignition switch and wiring for loose wires, burn marks, or other damage. Reconnect or replace as needed.

3. Use an ohmmeter to test continuity of the ignition switch and wiring. Replace defective parts as needed.

Hiring and Firing Ignition Parts

There are many other electrical components within your car's ignition system: sensors, a control module, and a distributor. Each can be tested using a volt-ohmmeter (VOM) and replaced as needed. It's critical that you compare the test results to those from the car's manufacturer.

To test and replace electronic ignition components, follow these steps:

1. Locate your car's distributor and electronic ignition, also called an ignition control module (ICM). The distributor operates from the camshaft, so it is mounted on the upper half of the engine. The ICM controls the ignition system and is mounted either within the distributor or nearby. Breaker-point ignitions are mechanically rather than electronically controlled.

2. Remove the distributor cap or ICM cover as necessary. Inspect the unit for obvious problems, such as a cracked cap or rotor, loose wires, or debris. Clean or replace as needed.

3. Following manufacturer's recommendations, use an ohmmeter to test continuity for each component. Find and test sensors as well as the ignition control module.

4. If necessary, remove and replace the distributor as a unit. Make sure that you note the rotor's exact position so that you can reinstall the new distributor with the rotor in the same position.

Chapter 10

Fuel and Exhaust System Repairs: What to Do About Gas

AAAAH!!

In This Chapter

➤ Safely repair your car's fuel-injection or carburetion system

➤ Replacing a defective fuel pump in four easy steps

➤ How to safely repair exhaust manifold and pipe problems

➤ Learn to replace your car's muffler and catalytic converter with basic tools

➤ How to repair your car's emissions control system

Where would your car be without a fuel system? Stranded!

Before you find yourself in this situation, you might want
to learn how repairs are done to an automotive fuel system. If not, at least read this chapter before you hire a mechanic to do the needed (or unneeded) repairs. You might
decide to do it yourself. Or, you might want to make sure
that the mechanic doesn't treat you like an idiot.

Your car's fuel system will be based on either a carburetor
or a fuel-injection system. One or the other. Which one?
If your car was built in the last dozen years, chances are
that it uses a fuel-injection system. If it was built before
then, it probably uses a carburetor. The car's owner's
manual and certainly its service manual will tell you
which you have.

In this chapter, you also will learn about repairs to fuel
pumps, fuel tanks, fuel lines, and exhaust systems (see the
figure illustrating the fuel system components). All cars
have these.

Unless you're Superman or Wonder Woman, you'll need
some tools to do these repairs. Chapter 2 covers basic repair tools and I'll try to identify special tools as we go
along.

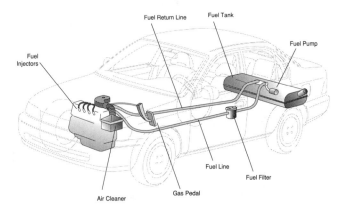

Components of an automotive fuel system.

Troubleshooting Fuel Failures

This section offers solutions to many common fuel system problems. Here are some additional tips:

➤ Are you sure that your car has gas? If you don't trust the fuel gauge, carefully lower one end of a cotton rope through the fuel filler pipe to test the depth of the fuel in the tank. A clean stick is better if it will negotiate all the turns in the filler pipe.

➤ If your car's engine starts OK but dies when you put it in gear, the carburetor (if it has one) may need the fast idle speed adjusted (see Chapter 5).

➤ If your car seems starved for fuel, remove the air filter. If the engine then runs smoothly, replace the air filter with a new one. If not, use a vacuum tester to test the fuel pump and fuel lines as covered later in this chapter.

➤ A vacuum leak in a fuel-injection system, intake manifold, or vacuum lines can cause all sorts of weird problems. Check vacuum hoses for leaks before repairing other parts (see Chapter 4).

➤ If your car runs erratically or not at all, check the fuel filter; if it is clogged, replace it.

➤ If your car sounds like a diesel engine when going uphill, buy a higher octane fuel or add an octane booster to your fuel tank (see your friendly auto parts retailer).

Painless Carburetor Surgery

The carburetor has been a vital part of a car's power system since cars first drank gas. The carburetor mixes fuel with air and sends it (through the intake manifold) to the engine cylinders for burning.

A carburetor is a mechanical device; it is not electronically controlled. That means it is subject to wear. Small jets get clogged with junk from the fuel tank. The float inside the carburetor's bowl or reservoir wears out or breaks. But, most often, poor fuel and too many gas additives take their toll on the carburetor, requiring that it be replaced. How can you tell? Troubleshooting tests (see Chapter 8) can help determine the source of the problem. If it is the carburetor, keep reading.

You have options. Sometimes, all your car needs is an adjustment or two (see Chapter 5). Because your carburetor is a mechanical device, you can rebuild it for less money than it costs to buy a rebuilt or new one. Or, you can whip out your wallet and plunk your money down for a new one. But, before you do, make sure that you've considered the other options.

Is rebuilding a carburetor difficult? Not particularly. In fact, the most difficult part may be selecting the right parts from the carburetor rebuild kit. These kits, available at auto parts stores for nearly all carburetors, typically are sold for more than one carburetor model. That means you're going to have some parts leftover when you're done. And instructions will be generic. One solution to this problem is to stay away from the low-price leaders at automotive superstores. If you're going to rebuild your car's carburetor, get a kit from the dealer's parts department or the original equipment manufacturer (OEM). It will cost more, but it will save you time. And time is money.

A carburetor is replaced following these steps:

1. Open your car's hood and look for the carburetor. In most cars, it is beneath a round metal part called the air-filter housing. Disconnect the large hose leading into the air-filter housing (if there is one) and

remove the nut on top of the housing. Disconnect any other parts and hoses needed to remove the air-filter housing.

2. You now should be able to see the carburetor. Disconnect the throttle linkage and the fuel line to the carburetor. You'll probably need the car's service manual as a reference so that you don't remove the wrong parts. Remember, the carb cops are watching you!

3. Remove the carburetor. For most cars, this means first removing the two or four nuts at the edges where the carburetor sits atop the intake manifold.

4. Remove the gasket between the carburetor and intake manifold. If the gasket lifts off easily, you're done. If it is stuck, you must scrape it off. To do so, first plug the holes on the manifold with rags so that bits of gasket don't fall in, making life more difficult. Then use a putty knife or other flat edge to remove all gasket material. (Don't forget to remove the rag from the manifold holes when you're done!)

5. Buy or rebuild the carburetor. You can buy a new or rebuilt unit, or you can rebuild it yourself with a carburetor kit. In general, rebuilding a carburetor means taking it apart, soaking parts in a carburetor cleaner, reassembling the parts, and adjusting them following the instructions in the kit.

6. Install the new or rebuilt carburetor in the reverse order of how you took it out. Install the new gasket, the new carb, attach lines and linkage, a new air-filter housing gasket, and then the old housing.

7. Finally, adjust the carburetor (if the manufacturer has provision for adjustment) following instructions in the car's service manual or in Chapter 5.

Messing with Fuel-Injection Systems

As you learned earlier, fuel-injection systems are more efficient and more trouble-free than carburetion systems. Even so, they may need periodic repair or replacement.

Most cars built since 1986 use fuel injection rather than carburetion. Some cars used it even before that.

The two most common types of fuel-injection systems today are throttle-body and multiport. There will be a quiz later, so pay attention—and drop that spitball!

A throttle-body fuel-injection system is similar to a carburetor, except that the amount of fuel is controlled electronically rather than mechanically. The fuel/air mixture then is distributed by the intake manifold to the cylinders. A multiport fuel-injection system electronically controls the distribution of fuel through one or more fuel rails (like pipes) to each cylinder's fuel injector. Multiport fuel injection (MPFI) also is called multiport injection, port fuel injection, and other creative names. Same thing.

Still awake?

So what can go wrong with a fuel-injection system? The system is controlled by the engine-control module (ECM) or the computer, which makes all the major decisions. So if the ECM is damaged, problems begin showing up in components it controls, including the fuel-injection system. Fortunately, these things don't fail very often, especially on newer systems in which the design bugs have been worked out. Unfortunately, when they do go awry, they go extremely awry—and even Einstein couldn't fix them. The solution then is to have a qualified and honest mechanic (I knew one once, but he died—broke!) test and replace as needed.

> **Mechanic's Tip**
>
> The best way to maintain your car's fuel-injection system is to make sure it drinks only quality fuel. Brand-name fuels today include additives specifically added to keep fuel injectors clean. If you suspect that your car's injectors are gummed up, try switching gas stations for a tank or two. Use fuel additives only if the gasoline you buy doesn't have them.

How can you tell if your car's fuel-injection system is sick? That's a toughie. Much depends on the type of fuel-injection system your car has, and whether other causes have been ruled out. Your car's service manual is the best source for specific ailments and cures. But, to understand them, let's look at typical fuel-injection system repairs.

I reiterate: Fuel-injection systems are complex. Tackle repair at your own risk. They can be repaired successfully by mechanically inclined car owners with a good service manual and the right tools. Really they can. Plan on spending some time scratching your head, however. A well-written service manual with lots of illustrations specific to your car's engine really makes the job easier.

Fuel injectors should last about 50,000 miles, and other parts in the system should last about twice as long.

Fuel-injection systems are repaired following these steps:

1. Relieve pressure in (depressurize) the fuel system. Fuel-injection systems are pressurized, so working on the fuel system requires that you first relieve system pressure. Your car's service manual or an aftermarket manual shows you how. Typically, you remove the filler cap on the fuel tank and then loosen the specified pressure reliever (a bolt or fitting).

2. Follow manufacturer's directions for testing and repairing or replacing components. Typical components include the air intake system, throttle body, fuel rail (MPFI), fuel pressure regulator, fuel injectors, and electronic control module. Sometimes you can fix a system simply by tracing down all the wires and hoses, attaching those that have worked themselves free or are damaged. Sometimes not.

3. If you are able to repair your car's fuel-injection system within reasonable time and cost, try not to act smug.

The Heart of the Fuel System

Fuel pumps use suction to pull fuel from the tank and deliver it to the carburetor or fuel-injection system. Older cars used mechanical fuel pumps that were operated by the engine's camshaft. Newer cars use electromechanical or solid-state fuel pumps. An electromechanical pump uses electricity to power the mechanical suction diaphragm. Solid-state fuel pumps rely on electronics to do the job and have no mechanical parts.

One more time: If your car has a fuel-injection system, make sure that you depressurize the fuel system before working on it. See the instructions provided earlier in this chapter.

To replace a fuel pump, follow these steps:

1. First, find the darn thing. Your car's fuel pump may be mounted on the side of the engine, somewhere in the engine compartment, near the fuel tank, or even inside the fuel tank. Your car's service manual helps you pinpoint it.

2. Test the fuel pump. Some fuel pumps can be tested without taking them off the car, whereas others

must be removed (see step 3). To test the pump, you first need to remove the fuel lines from the pump. Before disconnecting the input line, find a way of blocking it so that fuel from the tank doesn't spurt out. For a rubber input line, use Vise-Grip pliers to clamp the line. For a metal line, use a cap or a wad of putty to block flow after the input line is disconnected. Check input vacuum pressure with your finger or a vacuum gauge over the input. The car's service manual tells you what the input vacuum should be, but your finger over the input can give you a good idea as to whether the fuel pump is working. Check the fuel pump output pressure and volume in the same way.

3. To remove the fuel pump, remove the mounting bolts that attach it to the engine block, frame, or tank. Fuel pumps inside a fuel tank typically can be accessed through a cover underneath a back seat or a trunk mat. Disconnect any electrical wiring. Drain any gas in the fuel pump or bowl into a gas can. Remember: Smoking while you're working on the fuel system can really be hazardous to your health!

4. Replace the fuel pump with one of the same output. Your car's specifications will tell you what pressure and volume the fuel pump should be able to produce.

An Exhausting Tale

Where there's fire, there's smoke. The controlled explosions within your car's engine also produce "smoke" or emissions. Your car's exhaust system is supposed to remove these emissions from the engine and clean them up as much as possible before dumping them into the atmosphere. When your car's exhaust system doesn't do its job, you need to replace it.

Components in your car's exhaust system (illustrated next) include some or all of the following: exhaust manifold, exhaust pipe(s) and hanger(s), muffler, resonator, catalytic converter, and exhaust gas recirculation parts.

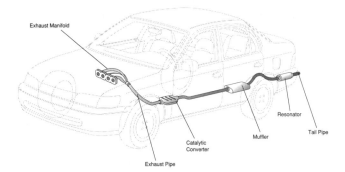

An exhaust system.

About replacing exhaust system components: some can be replaced with simply a wrench, whereas others require welding equipment. Assuming that you probably don't have an arc welder in your household (I could be wrong on this one), you can use clamps to cinch down joints between components. It's doable.

Working on your car's exhaust system typically means getting it up on safety stands or ramps, blocking the wheels, and crawling underneath. Sorry, it can't be helped.

Exhausting Troubleshooting Tips

In an effort to reduce noise and air pollution, here are a few tips for troubleshooting your car's exhaust system:

➤ If your exhaust system is loud, the muffler might need replacement. If the noise sounds more like hissing, it's probably a hole in an exhaust pipe.

➤ If the engine overheats or lacks power, the culprit might be a damaged muffler or tailpipe causing backpressure on the engine.

➤ If the exhaust system is noisy, visually inspect the pipes, muffler, catalytic converter, and other parts for obvious holes and broken hangers.

➤ If you can smell burning oil around the engine, the emissions-control system might be clogged and need cleaning or parts replacement.

The Manifold Life of an Exhaust System

As burned exhaust gases leave the engine's cylinders, they are collected by the exhaust manifold. The collected gases then are piped to the catalytic converter through the exhaust pipe. Cars with all cylinders in one row (2, 4, or 6) have one exhaust manifold. Cars with cylinders in a V-shape (V-6, V-8) have two exhaust manifolds. They're pretty simple in concept and construction.

So what can go wrong with an exhaust manifold? Not a whole heck of a lot. It can become cracked or warped from excessive engine heat. Look and carefully feel for exhaust escaping from places it didn't before. If so, the exhaust manifold may need to be replaced, although there are some aftermarket products that claim to repair manifold cracks. More often, repairing an exhaust manifold means replacing the gasket seals between the manifold and the engine block or the manifold and the exhaust pipe(s).

To repair an exhaust manifold, follow these steps:

1. When the engine is cold, locate the exhaust manifold on your car. The best way to do so may be backwards: Find the exhaust muffler and pipe under the car and trace it into the engine compartment where it attaches to the exhaust manifold.

2. If necessary, remove the bolts that connect the exhaust pipe(s) to the output of the exhaust manifold. You will need a long $1/_2$-inch socket wrench driver to loosen the bolts. If they won't budge, spray WD-40 or a penetrating lubricant on the nuts and let them sit for a while before trying again. After you have removed the bolts, check the gasket between the pipe and the manifold; if necessary, replace the gasket. Hold off on gasket replacement if you're also going to remove the manifold.

3. To remove the exhaust manifold, find and remove the bolts (or nuts) that attach the manifold to the engine block. There are typically two bolts per exhaust port or cylinder. Use a long $1/_2$-inch socket wrench driver to loosen the bolts or nuts. Carefully remove the exhaust manifold and gasket from the engine block.

4. Replace the gasket and/or exhaust manifold if either is damaged, making sure that the old gasket material is removed from the engine and manifold. Then reinstall the exhaust pipe to the manifold output, replacing the gasket.

Keeping Your Pipes in Good Condition

Exhaust pipes are simply round pipes that transport exhaust gases from the manifold to the catalytic converter and/or muffler. But these aren't pipes you can buy at a plumbing shop. Exhaust pipes are bent to fit specific cars. You can buy prebent exhaust pipes for most modern cars, or you can hire a muffler shop to bend the pipes.

To repair an exhaust pipe that has a hole in it, purchase and use a muffler repair kit by following the package's instructions. Most kits include a tape or adhesive that can temporarily plug the hole. Of course, don't bother repairing a pipe that has numerous holes and really should be replaced.

To replace an exhaust pipe, follow these steps:

1. If you are replacing the entire exhaust pipe, loosen and remove the bolts holding the pipe to the exhaust manifold, as described in the preceding section. If you are not replacing the entire pipe, loosen and remove clamps on the section(s) you will replace.

2. Carefully loosen and remove hangers holding the exhaust pipe to the underside of the car, making sure that the unit doesn't fall. You might need to grow or borrow an extra hand or two.

3. Replace the exhaust pipe(s) and reconnect to the system. If you also are replacing the catalytic converter, muffler, and/or resonator, do so as you replace the pipes, starting at the exhaust manifold and working toward the back of the car.

Mechanic's Tip

Apply anti-seize lubricant on threads when reinstalling bolts to make future removal easier.

4. You deserve a treat for such a nice job. Sorry, I don't have one for you, but you deserve it.

Silencing an Obnoxious Muffler

A muffler minimizes exhaust gas noises. So what does a resonator do? The same thing. Some cars have both a muffler and a resonator in the exhaust system to reduce noise. Other cars can get by with just a muffler.

To repair or replace a muffler or resonator, follow these steps:

1. Find and inspect the muffler/resonator for damage. A small puncture can be repaired using a muffler repair kit found at most auto parts stores. A rusty or damaged muffler/resonator should be replaced.

2. To replace a muffler/resonator, figure out how the old one was installed: by welding or by clamping. If welded, the exhaust pipe may need to be cut with a hacksaw or replaced. If the muffler/resonator's joints are clamped together with metal connectors, remove the nuts holding the clamp in place and remove the muffler from the pipe. You might have to remove one or more hangers from the pipe to free the muffler or resonator. Replacement parts are available at larger auto parts retailers.

3. Make sure that all clamps and hangers are tight before test driving your quiet car—or it may not be quiet for long.

How to Care for an Aging Catalytic Converter

If your car was born in the last 20-or-so years, it probably has a catalytic converter. There are two types: older ones reduce carbon monoxide and hydrocarbons; newer ones also reduce nitrogen oxides as well.

How long should a catalytic converter live? It should give you at least 50,000 miles of service and, with care, up to 100,000 miles.

If you suspect that the catalytic converter isn't working well, take it to a mechanic who has emissions-testing equipment. If your converter needs replacement, do so yourself or have it done. Don't even think about repairing a catalytic converter.

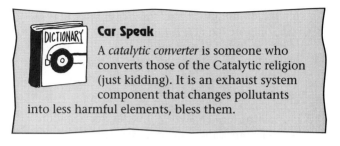

Car Speak

A *catalytic converter* is someone who converts those of the Catalytic religion (just kidding). It is an exhaust system component that changes pollutants into less harmful elements, bless them.

Also, make sure that your car hasn't been operated in at least eight hours, allowing the catalytic converter to cool down.

To replace a catalytic converter, follow these steps:

1. Find and inspect the catalytic converter. On most cars, it's located between the exhaust manifold and the muffler or resonator. Inspect it for obvious damage or simple solutions such as a loose clamp. A piece of wood can be carefully banged on the casing to test it for rust.

Mechanic's Tip

How can you keep your car's catalytic converter in top shape? Make sure your car uses only unleaded gasoline. Leaded gas and similar fuel additives can damage the catalytic converter and dramatically shorten its life. And you don't want to be responsible for that!

2. Remove the catalytic converter from the exhaust system. If the converter is welded, the exhaust pipe may need to be cut with a hacksaw or replaced. If your converter is clamped, remove the nuts holding the clamp in place and remove the catalytic

converter from the pipe. You might have to remove one or more hangers from the pipe to free the catalytic converter. Larger auto parts retailers and dealer parts departments can get you a replacement catalytic converter if you tell them the car's make, model, and engine size.

3. Install the new catalytic converter, replacing rusty exhaust pipes and hangers as needed.

4. Don't forget that converted catalysts also must be confirmed.

Controlling Your Car's Emissions

Your car probably has at least 1.625 scads of emissions-control devices hidden in its nooks and crannies (see the next figure), maybe more. What do these components do? The exhaust gas recirculation (EGR) system returns exhaust gases to the engine for reburning. The positive crankcase ventilation (PCV) system recirculates gases from the oil pan to the intake manifold. The evaporative emissions control (EEC or EVAP) system recycles fuel vapors.

It's AC (Acronym City) under your car's hood.

How can you repair these systems when they go awry? When you suspect—or have been warned by a state emissions control officer—that your car's emissions-control system isn't working efficiently, you can test and replace it. Your car's service manual or an aftermarket manual gives you specific instructions on how to test and replace these components. Here are some guidelines.

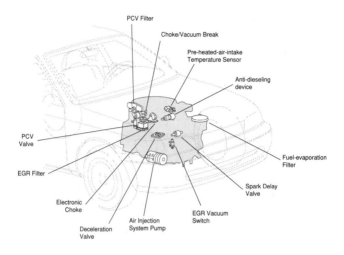

An emissions-control system.

To replace an emissions-control component, follow these steps:

1. Test the ECS components in your car using a vacuum gauge or volt-ohmmeter (VOM), depending on the component's function. If it is a sensor, a VOM typically tells you whether it's working correctly. If it recirculates fuel, oil, or emissions vapors, a vacuum gauge can register vacuum pressure. Compare readings with those suggested by the manufacturer.

2. Inspect the component for obvious damage. Then, clean it up and test it again. Vacuum-operated components can be cleaned with a solvent. Electronic components can be wiped clean and retested, but cannot be rebuilt. Instructions in the service manual overrule anything said here.

3. To replace a defective component, remove it from the car and take it (along with vehicle identification information) to your friendly auto parts professional. In most cases, the defective components are vacuum- or electrically controlled valves that either work or don't.

Car Speak

The *exhaust gas recirculation (EGR) system* recirculates exhaust gases to lower engine combustion temperatures and to reduce nitrogen oxides.

4. Install the new part and test the system to make sure that it works. Take your car to an emissions test center to verify that it works.

Chapter 11

Cooling and Lubrication System Repairs: Keeping Your Cool

UH-OH...

In This Chapter

➤ Repairing or delegating repair of the cooling system

➤ Replacing your car's water pump with basic tools and instructions

➤ Passing air conditioner repair off to experts who have the specialized tools and knowledge for the job

➤ Knowing how the lubrication system keeps your car's blood (oil) flowing smoothly

Most modern cars have a pressurized engine-cooling system (illustrated in the first figure in this chapter) that uses a thermostat to control the flow of coolant throughout the engine. The thermostat stops coolant from flowing until the engine is warm and then regulates the coolant temperature.

Why is the cooling system pressurized? Because the boiling point of a pressurized liquid is higher than that of one that is nonpressurized. So the engine can safely operate at higher temperatures without boiling over. Unfortunately, a pressurized system means that all parts, including hoses, must be strong enough to withstand the higher pressure.

The procedures in this chapter are typical for most modern cars. Refer to the manufacturer's manual or an after-market service manual for specific instructions and details.

As with other repairs, grab your handy-dandy car care toolbox. I'll let you know if there's anything special you need to make the repairs in this chapter.

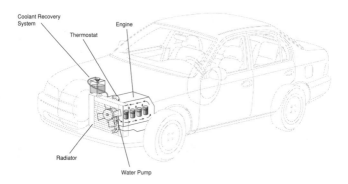

An automotive cooling system.

Troubleshooting Hot Cars

To make life somewhat easier, here are a few guidelines for troubleshooting cooling and lubrication systems:

➤ If your car always seems to run hot, first look for debris blocking the front of the radiator. Also check the seal on the radiator cap, test the radiator hoses (see Chapter 4), and then consider replacing the thermostat or water pump (covered later in this chapter).

➤ If your car warms up slowly, the thermostat may be stuck open.

➤ If you must remove the radiator from your car to have it rebuilt, consider buying a replacement unit instead. It might be cheaper.

➤ Check the sides of the engine block for signs of coolant leaking through round metal parts called freeze plugs or core plugs. Refer to the service manual for instructions on replacing core plugs.

➤ If you car's heater doesn't work after not being used for a while, find the heater under the hood or dashboard and check to see if the hose to it is attached to a spigot or valve that is closed.

If Your Car Is Radiating Too Much Heat...

Chances are you don't have the tools needed to repair your car's radiator. If it needs repair, the best you can do is remove it and reinstall it. Radiators for most modern cars are a commodity; you can order a new one through an auto parts store and pick it up on Tuesday. The price is cheaper if you bring your old radiator in for an exchange. Until you do, most auto parts stores or radiator shops require a deposit called a core charge.

To remove and reinstall a radiator, follow these steps:

1. Drain the car's cooling system as described in Chapter 7. If the coolant is relatively new and clean, save and reuse it. Some coolants can be poisonous to your pets.

2. If your car is equipped with an automatic transaxle, disconnect the coolant lines from the radiator.

3. Loosen the hose clamps on the radiator and detach the hoses. Some hose clamps require you to unscrew them, whereas others require you to use a special pair of pliers to squeeze the wires until the clamp opens.

4. Remove the engine cooling fan if it is attached to the radiator.

5. Loosen and remove the bolts holding the radiator to its frame.

Mechanic's Tip

Car coolant contains antifreeze that can be poisonous to pets. Some antifreeze products use toxic ethylene glycol and other ingredients that taste sweet. Newer antifreeze uses less-toxic propylene glycol. But check with the car's manufacturer to make sure using it doesn't void the car's warranty. Dispose of old antifreeze by sealing it in a leakproof container and taking it to a local recycling center.

6. Look around for any other components that are attached to the radiator and remove them. Mark their locations and sources to make reinstallation easier.

7. Lift the radiator from the frame, being careful not to spill coolant or to damage paint. Drain any coolant left in the radiator before taking it to the radiator shop or auto parts store.

8. Reinstall the radiator in the reverse order in which you took it out.

9. Refill the system with coolant, typically a 50/50 mixture of water and antifreeze.

10. Start the engine. As it is warming up, look for leaks.

11. To adequately test the new radiator, drive to an ice cream parlor at least 25 miles away, park and check for leaks, and then go in and order while the system is cooling. When your system is cool, check it again, get a quart to go, and drive home. Warning: Rocky Road is a bad omen!

Time to Take Your Temperature

If you suspect that the cooling system's thermostat needs replacement (because the engine is overheating), test some other options first before you start tearing into the engine. Check the coolant level in the reservoir or radiator (see Chapter 3). Check the tension on the engine drive belts (see Chapter 6). Make sure that the temperature gauge or warning light (see Chapter 8) is not the culprit.

To check the thermostat, let the engine run 15 minutes or more and then carefully place your hand on the hose that runs between the high side of the radiator and the engine. If the engine is hot but the hose isn't, the thermostat isn't doing its job. It needs to be replaced.

A thermostat can be replaced following these steps:

1. When the engine is cool, drain the cooling system. If the coolant is relatively new and clean, save and reuse it.

2. Find the upper radiator hose. Remove the clamp that attaches the hose to the engine.

3. Remove the thermostat housing from the engine block. It's typically attached to the block with two bolts.

4. Remove the thermostat from the housing, noting which way it is installed. Scrape away any gasket material on the housing or engine block using a screwdriver tip.

5. Install a new gasket, placing it exactly where the old gasket was. Make sure all bolt holes line up.

Mechanic's Tip

Don't run your engine without a thermostat. Bad things happen—and none of them are cheap to fix.

6. Install a replacement thermostat in the same way that the old unit was removed. Make sure that any pins or holes are lined up correctly.

7. Replace the thermostat housing.

8. Replace the upper radiator hose and clamp. If the hose will soon need replacement, save some trouble and do it now. Install a new clamp.

9. Refill the system with coolant.

10. Start the engine. As it is warming up, look for leaks. When the engine is warm, test the upper radiator hose for heat, as described earlier.

11. As needed, repeat step 11 of the preceding section for removing and reinstalling a radiator. Non-dairy treats are optional.

Improving Circulation

The water pump's job is to pump coolant through the engine and radiator. A water pump is actually a pretty simple part. A belt wrapped around the crankshaft pulley also turns the water pump shaft. Inside the pump, the shaft has a bunch of blades. As the shaft rotates, the blades go around, moving the coolant forward. It's more efficient than Congress—and easier to get good parts for!

The most common problem with a water pump is that the shaft wears out. On newer cars, there's a sealed bearing on the shaft. On older cars, the water pump has a zerk or lubrication fitting that needs a shot of grease once in a while. A water pump that is going out tells everyone so, making lots of racket and leaking coolant all over the place.

To replace a water pump, follow these steps:

1. When the engine is cool, drain the cooling system. If the coolant is relatively new and clean, save and reuse it.

2. Remove the drive belts and, if necessary, the timing belt (Chapter 6).

3. Remove any other parts attached to the water pump.

4. Remove the bolts holding the water pump in place. If one bolt is longer than others, make sure that you remember which hole it is from. Clean away any gasket or O-ring material on the housing or engine block.

5. Install a new gasket or O-ring.

6. Install the replacement water pump. Hand-tighten all bolts and then use a torque wrench to tighten them to the manufacturer's specifications.

7. Reinstall all parts removed to get to the water pump.

8. Refill the system with coolant.

9. Adjust the drive belt tension as described in Chapter 6.

What's the Condition of Your Air?

Stop! There are so many federal and state regulations limiting what a car owner can do to repair an automotive air-conditioning system that about all you can do legally is stare at it. The reason is that most older systems use a fluorocarbon-based refrigerant to cool the car's air (actually, it removes the heat from the air). None of us want fluorocarbons escaping into the atmosphere and eating up the ozone layer, so laws have been passed to make sure that only trained folks with approved equipment can work on automotive air conditioners.

Sorry.

But for you folks who want to know how it works anyway, the next figure might appease you.

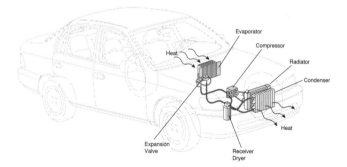

An air-conditioning system.

Keeping Your Car Out of the Junk Yard

Your car's lubrication system is simple. Oil held in the oil pan is pumped through the engine's oil passages. The oil pump does the work. If it doesn't, you've got a problem. Without lubricating oil, your car's engine soon becomes expensive scrap metal. So it's important to replace an oil pump that doesn't work properly before the engine is damaged.

So where the heck's the oil pump?

Good question! On some cars, the oil pump is located on the side of the engine. On others, it's in the oil pan (see the figure showing the lubrication system). After the oil pump is found and removed, you can repair it using a re-build kit available from a parts store, or you can buy a new or rebuilt one.

And why would you need to replace an oil pump? Because the car's idiot light or oil gauge says oil pressure is low, suggesting that the pump isn't working efficiently. Your car's owner's manual will tell you what normal operating pressure should be.

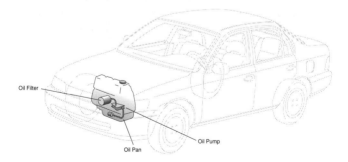

Oil Filter

Oil Pump

Oil Pan

A lubrication system.

An oil pump is typically replaced following these steps:

1. Check the service manual to locate the oil pump.

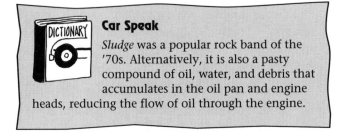

Car Speak

Sludge was a popular rock band of the '70s. Alternatively, it is also a pasty compound of oil, water, and debris that accumulates in the oil pan and engine heads, reducing the flow of oil through the engine.

2. If the oil pump is in the oil pan, drain the oil, re-move the pan and its gasket, and then remove the pump. If the oil pump is mounted on the side of the engine block, remove the bolts holding the pump in place, and then remove the pump.

3. Rebuild, repair, or replace the oil pump by following the manufacturer's instructions.

4. Replace the oil pump in the reverse order in which you removed it. If oil was drained from the oil pan, clean out any built-up sludge in the bottom of the pan, replace the gasket, and reinstall the oil pan.

Chapter 12

Steering, Suspension, and Brake System Repairs: Moving in the Right Direction

UH-OH...

In This Chapter

➤ How repairs are made to automotive steering and suspension systems

➤ How the car's front wheels are aligned for smooth steering and less tire wear

➤ How to replace shocks and struts yourself—or what to watch for when a mechanic does it

➤ Repairing your car's disc or drum brakes and saving yourself a hundred dollars or more in labor costs

➤ Learn to replace your car's master brake cylinder

➤ How to repair your car's power brake booster, if it has one

Your car's steering system enables the car to turn. Its suspension system smoothes out the ride. The brakes bring your ride to a smooth stop. It's that simple. Things can go wrong, however, making the ride rough, the steering difficult, or stopping impossible. In any of those cases, it's time to repair.

Let's tackle steering and suspension first, then brakes.

Many types of steering and suspension systems have been used to control cars. Until recently, most cars used pitman-arm steering, which passed the steering wheel's rotation to a lever (pitman arm) that moved side to side. Many of today's cars rely on rack-and-pinion steering, which uses meshed gears to control steering. Older cars use mechanical suspension that relies on springs and shock absorbers, whereas newer cars use hydraulic cylinders called struts.

All these components are covered in this chapter. Whether you do these repairs yourself or have them done for you, understanding what's involved will make you a smarter car owner.

What to Do When Your Car Wanders

Chapter 8 outlined how to troubleshoot common car problems. To add to your list of conversation starters, here are some guidelines for troubleshooting steering and suspension systems. Don't worry if you're not sure what all the terms mean as they are covered later in this chapter and in the glossary.

➤ If your car's power steering growls when you try to turn, first check the power steering booster fluid level. Then, if necessary, repair the power steering unit.

➤ If your car makes a high-pitched squeal, check the drive belt on the power-steering unit for slippage.

➤ If your car shimmies, check tire pressure and inspect the tires to make sure that they are all the same size and aren't damaged. Then check for worn tie-rod ends and lower balljoints in the steering system.

➤ If it is difficult to steer your older car, lubricate the steering system's zerk fittings to see whether that solves the problem before replacing parts.

➤ If your car leans hard on corners, check the stabilizer and struts for loose parts and wear.

➤ If your car shakes, shimmies, rattles, rolls, and gyrates, you have the Elvis Presley model.

Getting Wheels to Go in the Same Direction

Chances are that you don't have the tools and equipment in your garage to accurately align your car's wheels. You'll probably take it to a specialist who can do the job for you. Even so, understanding why and how wheels are aligned can help you better understand your car and help keep you from getting ripped off. You also can check tire wear to discover whether your car's wheels are aligned properly.

Maybe you've heard the terms *toe in* and *toe out* regarding wheel alignment. No, it's not a country line dance. The toe is the front edge of the wheel. Toe in means that the front edges of the two wheels are a little closer to each other than the heels or backs of the wheels. Toe out means the front edges are farther apart than the back edges.

Caster is the tilt of the steering connection to the wheel. *Camber* is the inward or outward tilt of the wheel's top.

Front-wheel-drive cars have different wheel-alignment specifications than rear-wheel-drive cars. The same is true

of front-engine and rear-engine cars. Your car's owner's
manual and service manual will give the manufacturer's
wheel-alignment specs.

Here are some tests you can make to ensure that your car's
wheels are aligned properly:

➤ Run your hand over the tire tread from the outer
   edge to the center and back to the edge. The surface
   should feel equally smooth in both directions. If the
   surface is rougher moving from the inner edge to
   the center, the wheel may have too much toe out. If
   the surface is rougher moving from the center to the
   outer edge, the wheel may have too much toe in.

➤ Wear on the outside edge of tires usually means that
   the camber isn't set properly.

➤ Wear on both inside and outside edges of tires usually means that the tire is underinflated.

➤ Wear in the center of tires usually means that the
   tire is overinflated.

Toe is corrected by adjusting the tie rod or rear lower arm.
Newer vehicles may have caster and camber set at the factory, with no adjustments available to the mechanic or car
owner.

Keeping Your Car in Suspension

Your car's suspension system (see the first figure in this
chapter) includes a shock absorber, a stabilizer bar, leaf
springs, a suspension arm, or MacPherson struts. These
parts wear out with use and need to be replaced. Here's
the lowdown on what each of them does:

> **shock absorber**   A mechanical cylinder that
> dampens a wheel's up-and-down movement caused
> by bumps in the road.

coil spring   A circular steel spring used to minimize up-and-down motion.

leaf spring   A group of flat steel springs used to
minimize up-and-down motion.

MacPherson strut   A component of most front-
wheel drive cars that combines the coil spring and
shock absorber into one unit; named for an engineer
at Ford in England—really!

stabilizer bar   Where you stop off before going
home after work; alternatively, a bar linking the
suspension systems on two wheels (front or rear) to
stabilize steering or turning.

independent suspension   A suspension system
that allows two wheels on the same axle to move
independently of each other.

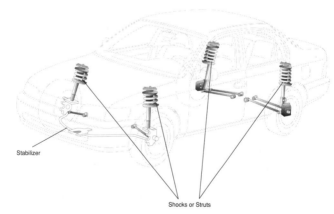

Stabilizer

Shocks or Struts

A suspension system.

How often do the parts in your suspension system need to
be replaced? Older cars may need new parts every 25,000
miles, whereas newer cars may go as many as 100,000

miles before needing parts replacement. Much depends on the car's design as well as how it is driven. Heavy loads and rough roads wear down suspension parts faster.

Because wear to suspension parts is gradual, you might not notice how far components have deteriorated. Steering becomes more difficult. The car doesn't corner as smoothly. Lots of passengers or heavy packages make the car sag more than it did. You can replace parts as recommended by the manufacturer, or you can test and visually inspect them using your car's service manual.

To replace suspension parts, follow these steps:

1. Find out what suspension parts your car has. A stabilizer bar buffers side-to-side motion. Shock absorbers and coil springs dampen up-and-down motion. A strut combines the shock absorber and coil spring. Front-wheel drive cars have suspension arms on the rear wheels.

2. Jack up the car and place safety stands under the wheels.

3. Cars with independent front suspension have a stabilizer bar. Stabilizer bars don't wear out; the rubber mountings, called bushings, do. The stabilizer bar and bushings are bolted to the underside of the vehicle between the right and left wheel suspension systems. Replace the bushings by removing the brackets holding the bar in place, removing the bushings, and replacing them. Stabilizer bar bushings are sold in sets at larger auto parts retailers.

4. Shock absorbers are installed inside the coil spring at each wheel. They can be replaced by removing the bolts at the top and bottom that connect them to the suspension system. Be sure to follow the

manufacturer's instructions because shock absorbers and springs are under tension and can injure you if they are not removed properly.

5. Struts are shock absorbers integrated into the coil spring. Remove the fasteners at the top and bottom that connect them to the suspension system. Your car's service manual or an aftermarket manual tells you exactly how. Don't try to disassemble a strut. Replace it as a unit.

6. Many cars have upper and lower suspension arms that allow the wheels to move up and down independently of each other. These arms typically don't need replacement, but the rubber bushings on which they are mounted do. To replace them, first locate and inspect them using the service manual. Most require that you loosen and remove a bolt on which the bushing is mounted.

7. Tell at least two people on the street about your experiences repairing your car's suspension system until tears come to their eyes.

The Steering Committee

A steering system (see the figure showing steering systems) uses a steering gear and rods to transfer the turning of the steering wheel to the front wheels. Steering gears usually last as long as the car, but some of the connecting components need replacement along the way.

Chapter 8 offers troubleshooting tips. Also refer to your car's service manual for specific information on fixing your car's steering problems.

As always, make sure that you install safety stands under your car before working there. Refer to your car's service manual for specific information on making repairs to the steering system.

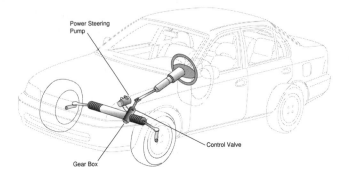

Power Steering
Pump

Control Valve

Gear Box

Pitman-arm and rack-and-pinion steering systems.

Steering systems are typically repaired following these steps:

1. Inspect, adjust, and, if necessary, replace tie-rod ends. Tie rods connect the wheels to the steering unit. The ends of these rods must be free to move with the movement of the steering system. They wear out. If they are worn or damaged, replace the tie-rod ends with ones from an auto parts retailer. Mark the exact location of the old ones so that the new ones can be installed in the same position and require little or no adjustment.

2. Check, adjust, and, if necessary, replace the steering gear unit. Many steering gear systems offer adjustments that can be made with a wrench and screwdriver while following instructions in the service manual. If replacement is needed, the steering wheel and column may need to be removed first. Each car is different, so check the manual for specific instructions.

3. Test the repaired steering system by driving to some friends' houses to tell them all about your repair

experiences. It helps if they're trying to watch a big football game.

Getting Help Steering

Some cars have a booster that uses hydraulics to make turning the steering wheel easier. Most power steering booster systems use a pump turned by the engine's crankshaft to circulate the hydraulic oil or fluid.

To repair power steering systems, follow these steps:

1. Check the power steering hoses for leaks or damage. A small leak can slowly drain the system of hydraulic oil and make turning the steering wheel difficult. Find the steering gear box (near the end of the steering column) and the power steering pump (on the front of the engine, driven by a belt). Locate the hoses running between the two units and check them for leaks and loose fittings. Replace them as needed with identical replacement parts.

2. If the power steering pump leaks or is noisy and must be repaired, loosen the bracket that maintains belt pressure, remove the drive belt, siphon fluid from the reservoir, and then remove the pump and reservoir. Have the unit rebuilt or replaced and reinstall it.

Car Speak

Power steering is a hydraulic unit that magnifies the driver's motions to more easily steer the car.

3. If power-steering fluid must be replaced or the reservoir is dry and fluid must be refilled, make sure you remove air from the brake system. Otherwise, air in the brake lines can make braking more difficult. Check your car's manual for specific instructions. In many cases, air can be removed from the power steering system by running the engine to operate the pump, removing the reservoir cap, and then turning the steering wheel fully to the left and then to the right a few times. Remember to replace the reservoir cap.

It Doesn't Stop: Brake System Repairs

Brakes are an obviously important part of your car. Although many car owners leave brake work to a specialist, it doesn't have to be so. Brake parts are commodities, easily found at larger auto parts stores. The steps to repairing or replacing brake parts are easy to follow. The job requires few special tools beyond those in your car care toolbox (Chapter 2).

Can you do the job as well as a brake specialist? Maybe not. But you can do it adequately—and sometimes better than a poorly trained employee who, last week, was grilling hamburgers. They know more; you know less. They have 100 brake jobs to do this week; you have just one.

Car Speak

Brakes convert kinetic energy into heat energy, slowing down the car. In an antilock brake system (ABS), an electronic system controls hydraulics to evenly distribute a car's braking power to avoid skidding.

Most cars today use a hydraulic brake system (see the figure below) with drum brakes on the rear, disc brakes on the front, and each with a brake cylinder that is controlled by the master cylinder. A hydraulic system uses brake fluid to force the brakes against moving parts in the wheels. Some cars have a proportioning valve that keeps the rear brakes from locking up when you slam on the pedal. Antilock Brake Systems (ABS) have a built-in proportioning valve and some electronics to control skidding.

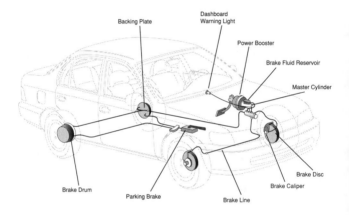

An automotive braking system.

Like more and more systems on today's cars, ABS is controlled by an electronic computer. Each brand is just a bit different to service. If your car has ABS, find and follow the service manual. ABS systems usually can tell you what's wrong with them through trouble codes. Deciphering these codes requires the service manual.

A word of caution is due. To work on your car's brakes, you'll have to jack up one or both ends of the car. Make sure that you place safety stands in the correct spots under

the car (see the owner's or service manual). Be safe, please!
I need to keep all my readers!

Troubleshooting Before You Hit the Skids

As promised, here are some useful tips for troubleshooting
automotive brake systems. Don't worry if you're not familiar with all the terms used here. You'll learn about
them later in the chapter. And you can find them in the
glossary.

➤ If your car pulls to one side during braking, first
check tire pressure and front-end alignment. Then
check for malfunctioning drum or disc brakes.

➤ If disc brakes squeal when applied, brake pads probably are worn out and need replacement.

➤ If the brake pedal pulsates when pressed, brake pads
or shoes may be worn unevenly and need adjustment or replacement.

➤ If drum brakes make a grinding noise, brake shoes
probably are worn out or the wheel cylinder is stuck.

➤ If the brake pedal seems mushy, there is probably air
in the hydraulic brake lines. Bleed the brake system
of air.

Replacing Your Car's Shoes

Most modern drum brakes (shown in the next figure) are
self-adjusting. When the brakes are worn, the drum brakes
need inspection and possibly replacement of key parts.
Brake shoes need to be replaced about every 30,000 miles.
You can do it.

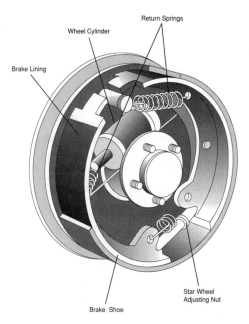

A drum brake system.

You need to be familiar with several parts of a drum system:

brake drum   The part on a drum brake system that receives pressure from the brake shoe.

brake shoe   The movable part of a drum brake system that applies pressure against the brake drum. The replaceable surface of a drum brake system is the friction lining, which typically is replaced with the shoe; alternatively, what brakes step on as they're dancing.

wheel cylinder   A hydraulic cylinder at each wheel that magnifies the master cylinder's pressure to evenly operate the wheel's brake system. Disc brake systems have wheel cylinders, too.

parking brake   A hand- or foot-operated brake that applies brake shoes or brake pads against the braking surface on a car's rear wheels; also called an emergency brake. All cars have an emergency brake.

What tools will you need for repairs in this chapter? The car care toolbox described in Chapter 2 will have most of the necessary tools. I'll mention any special tools as we go along.

To repair drum brakes, follow these steps:

1. Safely jack up your car and place stands under the axle.

2. Remove the wheel covers and then the wheel from the car as you would changing a tire (Chapter 3).

3. Remove the cap at the center of the axle using large pliers and/or a screwdriver. Remove the cotter pin by straightening the bent end and pulling the pin out from the round end. Remove the nut and washer.

4. Carefully pull the brake drum toward you, wiggling it from side to side if necessary to loosen it. The wheel bearings and washers will come off the axle first, so catch them in your hand and set them aside. Continue pulling on the drum until it comes off the axle, and then carefully set it aside.

5. Clean parts as needed with an old brush or com- pressed air so that you can see what you're doing. Caution: Older brake shoe linings use asbestos, so wear a filtering face mask when cleaning.

6. Inspect the inside of the brake drum for deep scratches, and the brake shoes and other parts for wear or damage. If in doubt about wear or damage, remove the part and show it to an experienced auto parts clerk.

7. To remove brake shoes, first install a wheel cylinder clamp (from the auto parts store) to hold the cylinder together. Then remove the large return springs using a brake spring tool (from the auto parts store, of course). Remove the self-adjusting unit as needed to free the brake shoes. Finally, remove any other fasteners or components holding the brake shoes in place.

Mechanic's Tip

To adjust a parking brake, press or pull the brake lever until it first clicks (about 1 inch). Then adjust the parking brake cable so that the brakes just start to drag on the rear wheels. The adjustment may be at the wheels or somewhere along the cable between the parking brake and the rear wheels.

8. Remove the wheel cylinder by disconnecting the brake line and removing fasteners holding the cylinder in place. If the cylinder is leaking or if you're completely replacing your brake system, replace the wheel cylinder with a new one. You can rebuild it yourself or buy a rebuilt unit.

Car Speak

The *brake caliper* part in a disc brake system squeezes the disc to make the car slow or stop. Calipers have a replaceable surface called brake pads. The pad wear indicator on the pad shows you when brake pads are worn to the point of needing replacement. Your car's service manual will tell you how to read the indicator.

9. Replace the brake shoes, wheel cylinder, springs, and other components as needed by reversing the earlier instructions.

10. Reinstall the drum, repack the wheel bearings (see the car's service manual), and replace the wheel and tire. When done repairing all brakes, refill the master cylinder with brake fluid and bleed the brake system, as described in your car's service manual. Finally, adjust the brakes if necessary (see the car's service manual).

11. Brag!

Replacing Your Car's Pads

Disc brakes (see the figure showing the disc brake setup) stop your car by applying lots of pressure to both sides of a spinning disc (rotor) on which the wheels are mounted. The brake pads are held and operated by the caliper, which squeezes the pads against the disc when you press your foot on the brake pedal.

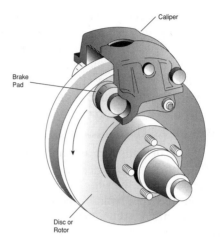

Caliper

Brake
Pad

Disc or
Rotor

A disc brake system.

Brake pads should give you at least 25,000 miles of service
before needing replacement.

To repair disc brakes, follow these steps:

1. Safely jack up your car and place stands under the
    axle.

2. Remove the wheel covers, and then remove the
    wheel from the car as you would while changing a
    tire.

3. Inspect the brake caliper, brake pads, the wear indi-
    cator, the disc, and other components of the disc
    brake system. If the brake pads are worn, replace
    them with new pads. They should be no thinner
    than $\frac{1}{16}$ inch. If the brake disc (rotor) is scored (has
    grooves in it), take it to a brake shop for resurfacing
    (turning) or replace it with a new disc.

4. To replace brake pads, use a C-clamp (which you can
    get at a hardware store or auto parts store) to push

the piston back in the caliper. Remove the bolt(s) holding the caliper in place and move it aside. Don't disconnect the caliper from the brake fluid line unless you plan to replace the caliper. If you do, brake fluid will leak out. Remove the brake pads and shims from both sides of the disc. Install new pads and shims following the instructions that come with the parts.

5. Reinstall the disc and hub assembly, repack the wheel bearings, replace the caliper and other components, and replace the wheel and tire. When done repairing all brakes, refill the master cylinder with brake fluid and bleed (remove any air from) the brake system, as described in your car's service manual or in the next section. Finally, adjust the brakes (see the car's service manual).

6. A fast-food test drive is optional, but highly recommended.

Masters of the Brake Universe

A brake system's master cylinder usually doesn't need replacement, except as an entire brake system is being rebuilt. You don't want a 15-year-old master cylinder trying to operate new wheel cylinders or calipers. If you replace wheel cylinders (done in pairs), consider replacing the master cylinder at the same time.

On most cars, the master brake cylinder is located on the firewall on the left (driver's) side of the engine compartment. Your car care toolbox (Chapter 2) will have the tools you need for this job.

To replace a master cylinder, follow these steps:

1. Remove fluid from the master cylinder using a siphon. Cover painted parts near the master cylinder with rags because brake fluid can damage paint.

2. Disconnect the brake lines from the master cylinder and plug the end of the lines to prevent leakage and contamination.

3. Disconnect the electrical wires from the master cylinder, marking them for later identification if it is not clear where they should go.

4. Remove the bolts holding the master cylinder in place and remove the unit from the car.

5. Replace the master cylinder with a new unit, reconnecting lines and wires. Refill the master cylinder with approved brake fluid.

6. Bleed the brake system following the manufacturer's instructions. Typically, this means having one person press on the brake pedal while another opens the bleed fitting on each wheel cylinder or caliper, in turn. Close the bleed fitting once brake fluid flows instead of air. Repeat the process at each wheel to remove air from the brake lines because air in the hydraulic system can reduce braking efficiency.

Getting Help Stopping Your Car

Power brake boosters make braking easier because they boost the driver's pressure on the master brake cylinder. Some power brake boosters offer adjustments that can be made as needed. Such adjustments can be made at the top end of the brake pedal before the brake pushrod goes through the firewall to the booster. Visually check your car's system for adjustments before replacing the booster. The car's service manual can tell you more—if there's more to tell.

Before replacing the power brake booster, test it to find the cause of the problem. Boosters that use a vacuum simply might have a hole or break in the vacuum line to the booster. Use a vacuum gauge to test the line following the manufacturer's instructions.

In addition, many power brake booster systems have an adjustable pushrod between the booster and the master cylinder. If your car has one of these, check the manual for information on this adjustment. You can save yourself some valuable time and money.

To replace a power brake booster, follow these steps:

1. Locate the power brake booster on your car. It typically is installed on the engine firewall between the brake pedal lever and the master cylinder.

2. If necessary, remove the master cylinder from the power booster. Depending on the system, you might not need to disconnect brake lines or drain the master cylinder; just remove the bolts mounting the cylinder to the booster.

Car Speak

The *power brake booster* is a hydraulic and vacuum unit that helps the brake's master cylinder magnify the driver's foot pressure to evenly operate the four wheel brakes.

3. Remove vacuum and hydraulic lines from the power brake booster unit, marking them for easier reinstallation.

4. Disconnect the power brake booster unit from the brake pedal arm. This typically means removing a nut or a cotter pin.

5. Remove the power brake booster unit from the firewall. On most cars, mounting bolts fasten the unit to the firewall.

6. Replace the power brake booster unit with an exact replacement, following instructions with the part or in the service manual. Some units require adjustments before installation, whereas others will be adjusted in place.

Car Speak Glossary

air cleaner   A metal or plastic housing on or near the carburetor or fuel injection intake with a filter to remove larger particles from the air.

alignment   An adjustment to keep parts in the correct relative position, such as the alignment of a car's wheels.

alternator   A component that converts mechanical energy into an alternating current (AC) that then must be changed (rectified) into a direct current (DC) for use by the car's electrical system.

antifreeze   A liquid added to water and used to keep a car's engine cool when running; the antifreeze ingredient keeps the coolant from freezing in cold weather.

anti-lock brake system (ABS)   An electronic system that controls hydraulics to evenly distribute a car's braking power to avoid skidding. See also *hydraulic*.

automatic choke   A device that reduces air flow into a carburetor when the engine is cold to increase the richness of the fuel/air mixture and help the engine start faster.

automatic transmission   A device that automatically selects gears based on the car's weight and speed.

ball joint   A ball and socket used as a joint in the steering arms, similar to a joint on a human body.

battery   A device that produces and stores direct current (DC) by converting chemical energy into electrical energy.

bearing   A part made of a metal and designed to reduce friction between surfaces.

bellhousing   A metal shroud that covers the engine's flywheel and the transmission's clutch or torque converter mechanisms. See also *clutch*, *flywheel*, and *torque converter*.

bore   The width of an engine's cylinder.

brake   A device that converts kinetic energy into heat energy, slowing down the car.

brake caliper   The part on a disc brake system that squeezes the disc to make the car slow or stop.

brake drum   The part on a drum brake system that receives pressure from the brake shoe. See also *drum brake*.

brake pad   The replaceable surface of a disc brake system's calipers. See also *disc brake*.

brake shoe   The movable part of a drum brake system that applies pressure against the brake drum; the replaceable surface of a drum brake system is the friction lining on the shoe.

camber   The inward or outward tilt of a car's wheel.

camshaft   The rotating shaft inside the engine that opens and closes valves using cams or rotating high spots.

carburetor   A device that dumps a stream of fuel into passing air for distribution to the engine's cylinders for burning.

caster   The backward or forward tilt of a car's front wheel axle or spindle.

catalytic converter   Someone who converts those of the catalytic religion; also, an exhaust system component that changes pollutants into less harmful elements.

CID (cubic inch displacement)   The total volume of all combustion chambers in an engine measured in cubic inches. To translate engine size from liters into cubic inches, multiply liters by 61.027.

clutch   A device that connects and disconnects the engine from the transmission, or an air conditioner compressor pulley from the compressor shaft.

combustion chamber   The area within an engine cylinder where combustion of a fuel/air mixture takes place.

compression ratio   The ratio of the area when a piston is at the top of its travel to that when it is at the bottom.

connecting rod   The rod that connects an engine's crankshaft to a piston. See also *crankshaft*.

constant velocity (CV) joint   A joint in a car's driveline that enables the shaft to pivot without vibration. See also *driveline*.

coolant   A mixture of water and ethylene glycol in a car's radiator that helps transfer the engine's heat to the air.

cooling system   The system that removes heat from the engine.

crankcase   The lowest part of an engine, surrounding the crankshaft.

crankshaft   The main rotating part of an engine that turns the piston's up-and-down motion into a circular motion that can be used by the transmission and, eventually, the wheels.

cylinder block   The largest part of the engine, including cylinders, oil passages, water jackets, and some other components.

cylinder head   The detachable part of the engine above the cylinders, sometimes including the valves or other components.

differential   The part of a rear-wheel-drive system that uses gears to transfer the driveline's power to two wheels as needed. See also *driveline*.

disc brake   A brake system that applies caliper pressure against a disc on wheels to stop the car. Typically used in the front wheels of many cars.

distributor   A device that sends the coil's electricity evenly and at precisely the right time to the engine's spark plugs.

drivebelt   The rubber and fabric belts that apply the crankshaft pulley's rotation to rotate an alternator, water pump, power steering pump, and air conditioning compressor, if so equipped. Some cars use a single belt, called a serpentine drivebelt, for driving many components.

driveline   The shaft and joints that connect the transmission with the differential. See also *differential*.

drivetrain   All components that transmit power to a car's wheels, including the clutch or torque converter, transmission, driveshaft, joints, and the differential or driveaxle.

drum brake   A brake system that applies brake shoes against the inside of a brake drum to stop or slow a car.

electrical system   The components that start your car, replenish and store electricity, and operate electrical devices.

electronic fuel injection (EFI)   A computer-controlled system that injects fuel into engine cylinders.

electronic ignition   An automotive ignition system that uses electronic signals to interrupt the electrical voltage within the distributor—common in cars built since about 1976.

exhaust emission control   One or more devices for reducing the engine's contaminants before they go into the atmosphere.

exhaust gas recirculation (EGR) system   A system that recirculates exhaust gases to lower engine combustion temperatures and reduce nitrogen oxides.

exhaust manifold   A system that collects exhaust gases from the cylinders and delivers it to the exhaust pipes.

filter   A replaceable part that attempts to keep contaminants out of the air, fuel, or oil used by an engine.

flywheel   A round metal wheel at the end of the crankshaft that collects and passes the engine's power to the transmission.

four-wheel drive   A drive system that distributes the engine's power to all four wheels.

front-wheel drive   A drive system that distributes the engine's power to the wheels at the front of the vehicle.

fuel   Any combustible substance that is burned to provide power or heat—for example, gasoline, ethanol, methanol, diesel, natural gas, or propane.

fuel/air mixture   The combustible mixture of gasoline fuel and air fed to an automobile engine.

fuel filter   A replaceable part that attempts to keep contaminants out of the fuel used by an engine.

fuel injection   Injects metered fuel into the intake manifold at each cylinder for burning.

fuel pump   A device that draws fuel from a tank and delivers it to the fuel system.

fuse   The weakest link in an electrical circuit, designed to fail first before an electrical overload damages other components.

fuse panel   A panel where electrical fuses are mounted for easy access.

gap   The distance a spark must jump between the center electrode and the ground electrode on a spark plug.

gasket   A thin, pliable material used as a seal between two metal surfaces.

ground   The neutral side of an automotive electrical system, typically the negative terminal, that is attached or grounded to the engine or frame.

horsepower   A confusing formula for determining the power generated by an engine.

hydraulic   A system that uses hydraulic oil to transmit or magnify power.

hydrocarbons   Any compound that has hydrogen and carbon molecules, such as in gasoline, diesel, or other petroleum products.

ignition coil   An electromagnetic device in a car that converts low voltage into high voltage.

ignition system   The system that supplies and distributes the spark needed for combustion within the engine.

independent suspension   A suspension system that allows two wheels on the same axle to move independently of each other.

intake manifold   A system that distributes air (port fuel-injected systems) or fuel/air mixture (carbureted and throttle-body injected systems) to the appropriate cylinders.

internal combustion   The combustion or burning of fuel in an enclosed area, such as an engine's combustion chamber.

leaf spring   A group of flat steel springs in a car's suspension system used to minimize up-and-down motion.

lifter   The metal part of a valve system between the cam lobe and the push rod or rocker arm.

liter   A measurement of volume equal to 61.027 cubic inches. To translate engine size from cubic inches to liters, multiply cubic inches by .0164.

lubrication system   The engine passages, the oil pump and filter, and related parts that lubricate the engine to reduce wear on moving parts.

Macpherson strut   A component found on most front-wheel drive cars that combines a suspension coil spring and shock absorber in one unit. See also *shock absorber* and *suspension*.

manual steering   An automotive steering system that doesn't use a power booster.

manual transmission   A transmission in which the driver manually selects the operating gear.

master cylinder   A hydraulic cylinder that magnifies the driver's foot pressure to evenly operate the four wheel brakes.

millimeter   A metric measurement equal to .03937 of an inch. There are 25.4 millimeters to an inch.

motor   An electromagnetic device such as a starting motor; technically, a car's power source is an engine rather than a motor.

muffler   A part that reduces the sound of automotive exhaust by passing it through baffles and chambers.

octane   A unit of measurement for a fuel's tendency to detonate or knock.

odometer A meter that reports miles driven since the car was built or since being reset at the beginning of a trip.

OEM (original equipment manufacturer) The maker of parts installed on the car when built.

oil pan The removable part of an engine below the block that serves as a reservoir for the engine's oil.

oil pump A part that pumps lubricating oil from the oil pan through the engine as needed to minimize wear.

overdrive A transmission gear designed to reduce engine speed and increase fuel economy when the car is operating at more than 50 miles per hour; some cars use a fifth gear instead of an overdrive gear.

overhead valve (OHV) engine An engine with the valves in the cylinder head instead of the engine block.

parking brake A hand- or foot-operated brake that applies brake shoes or brake pads against the braking surface on a car's rear wheels; also called an emergency brake.

passenger-restraint system A system of seatbelts and interlocks or internal switches designed to protect passengers from injury in an accident.

piston The movable floor of an engine cylinder that is connected by a rod to the crankshaft.

piston rings The rings that fit around the side of a piston and against the cylinder wall to seal the compression chamber.

pitman-arm steering A steering system popular for 50 years that used a gear to transmit the driver's steering motion to the pitman arm.

positive crankcase ventilation (PCV) A system of pipes and passages that recirculates vapors from the oil pan for burning by the engine.

power brake booster A hydraulic and vacuum unit that helps the brake's master cylinder magnify the driver's foot pressure to evenly operate the four wheel brakes.

power steering A hydraulic unit that magnifies the driver's motions to more easily steer the car.

rack-and-pinion steering A steering system with one gear across another, making steering more responsive than pitman-arm steering. See also *pitman-arm steering*.

radial tire A tire with cords or layers laid radially or across the bead; the most popular design today.

radiator A car part that reduces engine temperatures by transferring the heat in a liquid (coolant) to the air.

rear-wheel drive A drive system that distributes the engine's power to the wheels at the rear of the vehicle.

rocker arm A part of an overhead valve system that transfers upward motion of the lifters and/or push rod to downward motion of the valves. See also *lifter*.

rod bearing A dissimilar metal part between the crankshaft and individual connecting rods for reducing wear.

rotor (1) A brake disc on a disc-brake system; (2) A distributor part that rotates to transmit electricity to each spark plug wire through the distributor cap.

shock absorber A cylinder that uses hydraulic fluid to dampen a wheel's up-and-down movement caused by bumps in the road.

spark plug A metal-and-ceramic part that uses electricity to ignite the fuel/air mixture in the cylinder.

speedometer   A meter that indicates a car's speed by measuring the driveline's turning or rotation.

stabilizer bar   A bar linking the suspension systems on two wheels (front or rear) to stabilize steering turning.

starter   An electric motor that engages, spins, and disengages the engine's flywheel in order to start the engine. See also *flywheel*.

steering column   The shaft from the steering wheel to the steering gear.

steering system   A system of parts that transfers the turning movements of the steering wheel to the wheels.

stroke   The distance a piston moves up and down within an engine cylinder.

strut   See *MacPherson strut*.

suspension   The group of parts (springs, shock absorbers, and so on) that suspends the car's frame and body above the wheels.

thermostat   A heat-controlled valve that regulates the flow of coolant in an engine based on a preset minimum temperature.

tie rod   A jointed rod that ties the steering gear to the wheels.

timing gears   The gears that keep the camshaft (valves) in time with the crankshaft (pistons) using a timing chain or timing belt. See also *camshaft* and *crankshaft*.

torque converter   An automatic clutch on an automatic transmission. See also *differential* and *transmission*.

transaxle   A transmission and differential axle combined into one unit. See also *automatic transmission* and *clutch*.

transmission A component that transmits the engine's power to the wheels using gears.

tune-up A periodic adjustment and replacement of parts as recommended by the car's manufacturer.

turbocharger Uses a turbine to force more air into the cylinders to increase power.

universal joint A joint in a car's driveshaft that allows the shaft to pivot.

valve A part of an engine that opens and closes to control the flow of a liquid, gas, or vacuum. Most commonly, the intake valve lets fuel/air into, and the exhaust valve lets combusted gases out of, an engine's cylinder.

voltage regulator A device that regulates or controls the voltage output of an alternator or generator. See also *alternator*.

wheel cylinder A hydraulic cylinder at each wheel that magnifies the master cylinder's pressure to evenly operate the wheel's brake system.

wiring diagram A drawing depicting the electrical wiring and devices in a car—useful for troubleshooting electrical problems.

Zerk fitting A nipple-fitting installed to allow pressurized lubricating grease to be forced into a component.

Index

P-Q-R

W-X-Y-Z